CAPITAL
CONDENSED

A SHORT GUIDE TO MARX'S CAPITAL FOR OUR AGE OF GLOBAL CRISES

COLIN CHALMERS

Published September 2023 by Beachy Head Press
Registered in England and Wales as company 12598256
beachyheadpress.net

ISBN 9781838064631 paperback
ISBN 9781838064648 hardback
ISBN 9781838064655 ebook

Contents

Thanks
Introduction
1 Commodities and money
2 Capital and labour power
3 Exploitation
4 Productivity
5 Subsumption
6 Wages
7 Accumulation
8 Origins
9 Circulation
10 Turnover time
11 Reproduction
12 Profit
13 Competition
14 The falling rate of profit
15 Commerce
16 Interest and fictitious capital
17 Rent
18 Appearance and reality
Want to discuss *Capital?*
Categories
References

Thanks

I would like thank my fellow members of the *Capital* reading group at Pelican House, London for the discussions I have had with them while writing this book. In particular I would like to thank Seth Wheeler for his encouragement since I first suggested the idea of a short guide to *Capital* aimed at activists and Jamila Squire for her help in making it happen. I would also like to thank Cosmo, James Clammer and Michael Roberts for their comments on a draft. All errors are of course mine.

Most of all I would like to thank Alison Whiteoak for her encouragement while I wrote this book. Without it I would likely still be complaining that no one had.

Colin Chalmers, September 2023

Introduction

This a short book about three long books. Its purpose is to provide an understanding of what Karl Marx called the 'artistic whole'[1] of his writings as presented in *Capital* - the proposal that capitalism is a stage in history that creates the basis for a better world that we can only reach by moving beyond capital.

For some time humanity has had the capacity to produce enough wealth to meet everyone's needs in an equitable and sustainable way. Instead, we find ourselves hurtling towards catastrophe, apparently unable to change course. Human use of fossil fuels is warming our planet with disastrous consequences. Human exploitation of nature is reducing biodiversity through soil depletion, deforestation, overfishing and the destruction of numerous habitats.

The ecological systems that maintain the narrow limits within which human and other life on earth can survive are being systematically weakened as we head towards ecological tipping points that will drastically change our climate for the worst, quickly.[2]

We know what needs to be done to avoid disaster. But we don't do it. Oil companies keep expanding fossil fuel production, making huge profits in the full knowledge of what their actions mean for the world. Other companies ravage nature with no thought for the long-term damage they cause. Governments keep letting them.

What is it about our world that makes humanity act in ways that are obviously against its own interests? If we replace our current politicians with better politicians will things get better? Or is something more fundamental at work?

Marx wrote *Capital* to answer these questions. He argued that capital, the value capitalists accumulate by exploiting workers, cannot help but grow, whatever the cost to people or planet. This ecocidal process of expansion has created a world run by the need to make profit whatever the cost to human wellbeing or ecological health.

Capital is more a book about ecology than an economics book. It is a critique of the economists' assumption that commodities, money and profit are as natural as clouds, hills and oceans. Economics takes the existence of class society, where a few people own the factories and fields that produce what we need and the rest of us have to work for them, as inevitable, natural and fair to all.

This is what *Capital* challenges. If ecology is the study of the fundamental relationships between humanity and the rest of nature then *Capital* is an ecology book.

Capital is divided into three volumes and 18 parts (some parts have been renamed in this book for clarity. Texts in quotation marks are quotes from the relevant part of *Capital* in its original English translation at the online *Marxists Internet Archive*).[3]

Marx started his scientific investigation into capital by gathering empirical evidence about capitalist society in order to understand its underlying laws. He did this by

abstracting the fundamental **categories** of capitalism and seeing how they relate to each other (when a word or phrase is in bold it introduces a new category and links to *Categories* where the meanings of categories are listed).

The presentation of this investigation in *Capital* begins with the most basic category in capitalist society, the commodity.

Capitalism grew out of commodity production, which itself grew out of the exchange of products between early human communities. Communities producing more than they needed of some things exchanged this surplus with other communities for things they did not have but wanted.

For this exchange to happen there had to be a way of deciding how much of one product should be exchanged for an amount of another product. This is how commodities were born.

Marx shows how the **contradiction** within the commodity between being something that is useful and something that must be sold before it can be used implies the existence of other categories like money. As *Capital* progresses, new categories like capital, profit and interest are introduced until we arrive at a description of how capitalism appears to us in everyday life.

This is not a description of a static system. Capital must grow, and nothing can grow forever. By increasing what humans are capable of and connecting the world, capital creates the conditions for **socialism** or communism - Marx used the terms interchangeably - a classless society where production is run by **associated producers** for need, not profit. *Capital* shows the possibility and necessity of getting there.

Many people want to stop climate change, ecological

destruction, exploitation and poverty by taming capital, making it work in the interests of the majority rather than a small minority. They argue for progressive governments that would improve the way capitalism works by increasing public investment, taxing the rich more, improving social welfare and taking an enlightened approach to climate change. If these people are right, and capitalism can solve our present crises by changing government policies, there is no need to abolish capital.

What *Capital* shows is that this is an impossible dream. Fighting for social justice and action on our climate emergency can win real victories, but as long as the capitalist relationship between workers and capitalists remains the fundamental relationship in a society those victories will be followed by greater defeats.

By showing how capital came into being and develops according to laws that cannot help but cause ecological destruction, inequality, debt and unemployment, *Capital* shows that until we take control of production away from capitalists, the crises caused by capital will cause disaster for billions.

Capitalism is not as universally accepted as you might think from consuming the capitalist-owned media. There are mass movements across the world challenging capitalist exploitation and destructiveness who see capital as the obstacle to a better world. A 2020 survey found that 56% of the world's population believe capitalism is doing more harm than good.[4]

History, like ecology, has tipping points, when popular opposition to rulers can change societies fundamentally. As Ursula K. Le Guin has pointed out 'We live in capitalism. Its powers seem inescapable. But then so did the divine rights of kings'. *Capital* shows that capital plays a transitory role in history between class society and a classless one, that another world is possible if we move beyond capital and that doing that is the task of our time in history.

1 Commodities and money

Any society where people produce things of use to each other produces and consumes **wealth**. In **capitalist societies** this wealth appears as 'an immense accumulation of commodities' being produced, sold, bought and consumed. Our investigation therefore begins with an analysis of the **commodity**.

Every commodity has a dual nature. On the one hand, it has a **use value** because it is useful in satisfying a human want. This use value is the commodity's **natural form** because the commodity would satisfy human wants in any society where **products** of human labour are produced and consumed.

On the other hand, it also has an **exchange value** because, as a commodity, it must be exchanged before it can be consumed. Its exchange value is its **social form** because products of human labour only have an exchange value in societies based on **commodity production**, production for **exchange**.

If we leave out of consideration commodities' various use values, the property commodities have in common is that human **labour** has been spent producing them. This labour gives commodities their **value**. This value, how much a commodity is worth, can only be expressed in terms of the use value of another commodity, for instance a table being worth four chairs. The ratio in which a commodity exchanges with another commodity is its exchange value with that commodity. The exchange value of a commodity expresses its value, the amount of society's labour it represents.

This dual nature of commodities as something both useful and having value, reflects the dual nature of the labour that produces them. On the one hand labour is specific, useful, **concrete labour** that produces a specific use value. On the other hand it is the expenditure of human labour as such, **abstract labour**, a part of society's total labour.

The value of a commodity depends on the amount of abstract labour contained in it measured in time. This does not mean that the slower or less efficiently labour is carried out the more value is created. The value of a commodity is determined by the normal amount of labour time it takes to produce it in a particular society at a particular time, the **socially necessary abstract labour time**, rather than the amount of concrete labour it actually takes to produce. This is why the **law of value** states that a commodity's value is determined by the socially necessary abstract labour time needed to produce it.

Different concrete labours need different **skills** and abilities that take different amounts of labour to teach and learn. An increased **intensity of labour** creates more commodities and more value in the same time than labour of average intensity. More skilled and intense labour count as multiples of **average labour**. We assume for our investigation that all labour is average labour.

Humanity is part of **nature**. In any society nature is the basis of human life and the primary means of meeting human needs. However, despite producing immense use values, most basically the planet we live on and the air we breathe, the use values created by nature have no value and add no value to commodities because no human labour has been spent producing them. Value is a relationship between people, not a measure of usefulness. Products of labour that someone produces for their own consumption, say food grown and consumed by its grower, have no value. Products that are useless have no value either, as commodities must have a use value as well as a value.

Value is not an accurate measure of wealth. As commodities produced with the same amounts of socially necessary labour time have the same value, if someone finds a way to half the labour needed to produce a table then twice as many tables can be produced in the same time as before with the same labour, halving the value of each table produced. The same amount of labour always produces the same amount of value. When the **productivity of labour** increases, the same amount of labour produces more use values in a given length of time, reducing the value and exchange value of each commodity produced.

The total labour of any society is divided into a range of concrete labours producing a range of useful products to satisfy a range of human wants. In societies based on commodity production, a complex, ever-changing **division of labour in society** develops spontaneously, operating independently of anyone's will, where the **private labour** of individual **producers** only becomes **social labour** through the exchange of privately produced commodities, a relationship between things rather than people.

The facts that commodity producing labour is not

directly social and that the exchange of commodities takes place beyond the control of anyone's will create **commodity fetishism**. Socially exchanged commodities produced by private labour 'appear as independent beings endowed with life' with power over people in the same way as many religions see gods having power over people, acting in mysterious ways that we cannot understand but must adapt to.

Commodity fetishism has its origin 'in the peculiar social character of the labour that produces [commodities]'. 'The equality of all sorts of human labour is expressed objectively by their products all being equally values; the measure of the expenditure of labour power by the duration of that expenditure, takes the form of the quantity of value of the products of labour; and finally the mutual relations of the producers, within which the social character of their labour affirms itself, take the form of a social relation between the products'.

The value of a commodity can only be measured in terms of the use value of another commodity. If the value of a table is measured as four chairs, the chairs become the things that the table's value is expressed in. A table is worth four chairs.

A commodity has the **relative form of value** when expressing its value and the **equivalent form of value** when it is the commodity in which another commodity's value is expressed. The amount of concrete labour producing the chairs, the equivalent commodity, becomes the medium for expressing the abstract labour contained in the table.

As the variety of commodities grows, it becomes increasingly difficult to measure each commodity against every other commodity. The pressure for a **universal**

equivalent to all other commodities grows until a single or a few commodities become this universal equivalent, the **money** commodity against which other commodities are measured. The most common commodities to take on this role are the precious metals because they are inert, of high value and can be easily divided and reunited. More than any other commodity, **gold** becomes money. We will assume that gold plays this role of **money material** rather than silver, diamonds or other commodities that can play this role.

The exchange value a commodity has with gold as money becomes its **price** measured in a quantity of gold. Every commodity becomes worth a certain amount of gold. Gold as money becomes 'the socially recognised incarnation of human labour'. Instead of our table being worth four chairs because its value is four times that of each chair, it is now worth four times as much gold as each chair. This is the first function of money, as the universal **measure of value** that allows commodities to express the amount of socially necessary labour time they contain ideally by their price. The commodity's value is expressed in the only way it can be, as having an exchange value equal to a certain amount of another commodity, being worth a certain amount of money. Money functions here as a **standard of price**, a fixed amount of money a commodity is worth.

As soon as producers give their commodities prices, the necessary relation between labour and value becomes an exchange relation between one commodity and another, the money commodity. This exchange relation allows a commodity's price to go up or down without its value changing. The possibility of price deviating from value 'admirably adapts the price-form to a mode of production whose inherent laws impose themselves only as the means of apparently lawless irregularities that compensate one another'.

Commodities sell at prices, not values, because prices are measured in money, while value is measured in labour. When a commodity takes the same amount of labour to produce as the gold representing its price, it is sometimes said to sell at its value but this is more accurately described as selling at its **direct price**. Although in reality commodities rarely exchange at their direct prices, assuming they do is an abstraction that helps us investigate how capitalism works. Apart from the discussion of competition at the beginning of *Part 4 Productivity*, we assume commodities sell at their direct price until *Part 13 Competition*.

Things that have not been produced by human labour but can be bought and sold, from uncultivated land to someone's vote in an election, can take on the form of commodities. When something has a price without having a value its price is an **imaginary price**.

Commodity producers sell the commodities they produce to get money to buy other commodities they need. This can be expressed as a circuit of commodities (C) to money (M) to commodities (C) or, using these symbols to represent exchanges, C-M-C. Each purchase (M-C) is at the same time a sale (C-M) in another circuit.

The circuit made by one commodity is inextricably connected with the circuits of other commodities. The total of all these different circuits constitutes the **circulation of commodities**. As the circulation of commodities involves buying and selling, the exchange of commodities for money, it entails the currency or **circulation of money** in the opposite direction, with

money acting as the **means of circulation** of
commodities.

The total price of all commodities sold is the same as
the money that buys them. Some commodities sell faster
than others so the money used to buy them circulates
faster too. The average number of moves made by money
in a particular period is the average speed of the circulation
of money. The total price of all commodities sold in a
period of time is equal to the total **quantity of money** in
circulation multiplied by the number of times the money
circulates.

If a producer sells more commodities than they buy (C-
M without M-C) they accumulate a **hoard** of money that
can be spent in the future. The ability of money to be
hoarded allows the amount of money in circulation to
expand and contract. If producers cannot find buyers for
their commodities (M-C without C-M) the circulation of
commodities and money stalls and a **crisis** can develop.
We will see how this possibility of crisis inherent in
commodity production develops into crises in capitalist
societies in *Part 14 The falling rate of profit.*

There is no need for actual gold to be exchanged when
people buy and sell commodities. Symbols of money that
can be exchanged for gold are able to perform this
function of money just as well. Gold coins are replaced by
token money in the form of coins made of cheaper metal,
then pieces of paper, objects with little or no value
themselves but a much more practical way to pay for most
commodities than actual gold.

'The function of gold as coin becomes completely
independent of the metallic value of that gold. Therefore
things that are relatively without value, such as paper
notes, can serve as coins in its place. This purely symbolic

character is to a certain extent masked in metal tokens. In paper money it stands out plainly'.

States issue token money, sometimes called **fiat money,** in the form of **national currencies** to represent money within their national boundaries. The way these currencies exchange for commodities has developed from coins, **banknotes** and cheques to cards, touch payments and phone apps without changing their role as token money.

Token money is subject to the same laws as money itself 'only in so far as paper money represents gold, which like all other commodities has value, is it a symbol of value'. If a state issues more token money than the amount the gold which would circulate if not replaced by token money, the value of its national currency falls.

Credit results from the circulation of money and money's function as a **means of payment**. As some commodities takes longer to produce than others, some producers find themselves needing other producers' commodities before they have the money from selling their own commodities to buy them. These producers are given credit, allowed to receive commodities before paying for them in return for agreeing to pay the **debt** in the future. They become a **debtor** while the lender becomes a **creditor**.

As credit expands and is used in more and more transactions, a continuous **circulation of credit** develops alongside the circulation of commodities and money. The existence of credit, where strings of debts cancel each other out without any money changing hands, means that the amount of money and commodities circulating each day no longer correspond.

The exchange of commodities breaks through all sorts of boundaries as it 'develops a whole network of social relations' that are 'spontaneous in their growth and entirely beyond the control of the actors'. Gold remains the medium for international payments between national currencies, the universal **world money** in the **world market**, the worldwide medium of payment and embodiment of wealth. 'It is only in the markets of the world that money acquires to the full extent the character of the commodity whose bodily form is also the immediate social incarnation of human labour in the abstract'.

Since the mid-20th century, the United States' dominance of the world economy has made the US dollar a token for world money. The United States has been the world's largest economy since 1871,[1] has more than twice the gold reserves of any other country[2] and is responsible for 39% of the world's military spending.[3] Although the US accounts for less than a quarter of world production[4] the US dollar's role as the representative of world money means that 85% of foreign currency transactions are carried out in US dollars.[5]

As long as the US government can maintain the US dollar's role as a token for world money, it can run up colossal debts in the knowledge that the rest of the world will continue to demand their dollars. The current dominance of the US dollar is not assured and does not change the fact that it is token money that in the last resort is only a symbol of the money commodity, gold.

Classical political economy or **classical economics** was a scientific attempt to understand how production is regulated in commodity producing societies. Classical economists such as Adam Smith (1723-1790), the founder of economics as a science, and David Ricardo (1772-1823) who 'gave to classical political economy its final shape'[6] recognised that commodities had use values and exchange values and that labour produced value. However they also accepted the fetishistic illusion that humans will always relate to each other through the exchange of privately produced commodities.

Karl Marx (1818-1883) gave *Capital* the subtitle *A Critique of Political Economy* because he saw it as an investigation into the limits of classical economics' understanding of capitalism. While Smith and Ricardo saw capitalism as a natural fact of human existence, Marx's development of the law of value in *Capital* shows capitalism to be a stage in the development of human society that is ripe for change, something classical economics could not contemplate.

From the middle of the 19th century, what Marx called vulgar economics and is nowadays called **mainstream economics** began to replace classical economics. Mainstream economics rejects the possibility of understanding how commodity production works altogether, offering a description of the appearance of economic relations instead.

Within four years of the first volume of *Capital* being published in 1867, mainstream economics was replacing the law of value with the view that value arises from the subjective experiences of consumers rather than from human labour.[7]

This is the economics taught in schools and colleges, an ideology that sees capitalism as the best of all possible worlds, inevitable rather than temporary, rational rather than fetishistic, the end of history rather than, as *Capital* shows it to be, a stage in history that prepares the ground for humanity taking control of its own destiny.

2 Capital and labour power

We have seen that the circulation of commodities, C-M-C, means people selling commodities so they can buy different commodities. For commodities to circulate money has to circulate too. As the means of circulation, money keeps circulating while commodities step in and out of circulation to be consumed and replaced by new commodities.

As the production of commodities grows, the amount of money in circulation grows too and appears to develop 'a life-process of its own'. Value circulating as commodities then money then commodities again becomes value in process, money in process, self-expanding value, and as such **capital**.

Money becomes capital when the circuit C-M-C, selling in order to buy, develops into the circuit M-C-M', buying in order to sell, with money thrown into circulation to extract a larger sum of money out of it. 'In the one case both the starting-point and the goal are commodities, in the other they are money'. M-C-M', is the **general formula of capital in circulation**.

While the simple circulation of commodities, selling what you make in order to buy what you need, is a means of satisfying wants, 'the circulation of money as capital is, on the contrary, an end in itself, for the expansion of value takes place only within this constantly renewed movement. The **circulation of capital** has therefore no limits'. Capital is an algorithm for the limitless growth of value, one that tries to break through any **social limits** or **natural limits** put in its way, whatever the cost to humanity or nature.

How do capitalists turn money into more money? The earliest capitalists were traders and money lenders who built up their capital by selling or lending at a higher price than they bought or borrowed. Gains made in circulation are always someone else's loss so these transactions only redistribute value and cannot explain how value is created.

The sole source of the extra value created in the circuit M-C-M' is the commodity **labour power**, the only commodity with the use value of being able to produce value. Labour power is human creativity, 'the aggregate of those mental and physical capabilities existing in a human being, which he exercises whenever he produces a use value of any description'. Capital can only expand by turning this ability to labour into a commodity which the **worker** has to sell to the **capitalist** for periods of time in order to live. When workers do this, they **alienate** their labour power, allowing their labour to become part of capital. The alienation of labour power, labour power becoming labour, value being created and commodities being produced are the same thing and constitute **capitalist production**.

'As the conscious representative of this movement, the possessor of money becomes a capitalist'. The expansion of value becomes the capitalist's subjective aim and 'it is only in so far as the appropriation of ever more and more wealth in the abstract becomes the sole motive of his operations, that he functions as a capitalist, that is, as capital personified and endowed with consciousness and a will'.

We saw in *Part 1 Commodities and Money* that the value of a commodity is determined by the amount of labour needed to produce it. Once human creativity becomes the commodity labour power, the **value of labour power** becomes the labour needed to produce that labour power, the worker's **means of subsistence**. The worker's means of subsistence include food, clothing and the normal necessities of life as determined by what society finds acceptable.

The worker, or someone else in the worker's home, needs to clean, cook, shop and carry out other tasks to be able to reproduce their labour power each day and bring up the next generation of workers. **Domestic labour**, usually carried out by women, is labour carried out privately in the household that is necessary for labour power to be reproduced, and therefore necessary for capitalist production, but produces no value itself. Like so much else, it is a free gift to capital. The dual role women play as the main providers of domestic labour and as workers with less secure and worse paid jobs than men is the basis of **women's oppression** under capitalism.

3 Exploitation

'Capital is dead labour, that, vampire-like, only lives by sucking living labour, and lives the more, the more labour it sucks.'

In any society the **labour process** is purposeful human activity that creates useful products by interacting with **objects of labour**. Some objects of labour, such as the soil, are provided free by nature. Objects of labour that are the product of previous labour provide the **raw materials** and **intermediate goods** out of which new commodities are produced.

During the labour process, humans interact with the objects of labour using their own bodies and **instruments of labour,** originally simple tools. As with the objects of labour, some of these instruments of labour are provided spontaneously by nature. Objects and instruments of labour that have been changed or produced by previous labour are called **means of production**.

The aim of the labour process in capitalist production is not to produce useful products, it is to produce more value than the individual capitalist invests, contributing to the **self-expansion of capital**. 'The life-process of capital consists only in its movement as value constantly expanding, constantly multiplying itself'.

The process of capitalist production begins when a capitalist uses money they own as their **original capital** to buy labour power and means of production of the kind needed to produce a particular kind of commodity. The capitalist then consumes the workers' labour power in the labour process by bringing it together with means of production and free gifts of nature so that the worker's **living labour** produces new commodities and new value out of them. At the same time as creating new value, living labour transfers the value of the **dead labour** embodied in the means of production used up during the labour process. Once commodities have been produced, they belong to the capitalist.

The dead labour contained in the objects of labour transfers all its value to the commodities being produced. The tools, machines, buildings and other means of production used in the labour process that do not transfer all their value to each commodity transfer their value to produced commodities over a period of time.

The value of the dead labour embodied in the means of production remains constant during the labour process so the means of production are called **constant capital**.

Labour power is the only commodity with the property of being able to create more than its own value during the labour process so the living labour power used in production is called **variable capital**.

Capitalists only produce commodities because they contain more value than the value of the capital used to produce them. The difference between the value of a commodity and the value of the means of production and labour power consumed in producing it is **surplus value**,

value created by workers which belongs to capitalists. The creation of surplus value is the purpose of capitalist production.

Where does this surplus value come from? The labour carried out during the **working day** is made up of paid or **necessary labour time** when commodities with the same value as the worker's means of subsistence are produced or **surplus labour time** when workers produce surplus value for the capitalist. For capitalist production to take place there must be **necessary labour** for workers to survive and reproduce and **surplus labour** producing surplus value for capitalists.

The value of any commodity consists of the value of the dead labour contained in the constant capital (c), the value of the workers' labour power (v) and the surplus value (s) created by workers, c + v + s.

The **rate of exploitation** or rate of surplus value is the ratio between the surplus value and the variable capital contained in the produced commodity, s / v. It expresses the ratio between the amount of value produced in the labour process going to capitalists and the amount going to workers. If the rate of exploitation is 100%, the surplus value will be the same as the variable capital.

The **mass of surplus value** produced is equal to the variable capital times the rate of exploitation. A fall in the rate of exploitation will not reduce the mass of surplus value if the number of the workers employed or the amount of labour each worker carries out increases enough to compensate for the reduction.

The fact that surplus value is only created by living labour seems to contradict reality. Capitalists who employ more constant capital per worker make their workers more productive and seem to produce more value per worker than capitalists who less constant capital per worker. This apparent contradiction between the law of value and how things appear in everyday life is resolved in *Part 13 Competition.*

Capitalists extend the working day as far as they can, treating workers solely as a source of surplus value so 'food is given to the labourer as to a mere means of production, as coal is supplied to the boiler, grease and oil to the machinery.'

'All this does not, indeed, depend on the good or ill will of the individual capitalist. Free competition brings out the inherent laws of capitalist production, in the shape of external coercive laws having power over every individual capitalist'.

There are natural limits to the hours a worker can labour each day. The working day cannot be longer than 24 hours and workers must have time for sleeping, eating and the recreation of their labour power. There are also social limits to the length of the working day based on what society considers acceptable.

In all societies where **classes** exist, they compete with each other through **class struggle** over who receives the fruits of labour and which class organises production. In capitalism, one form the class struggle between the **capitalist class** and the **working class** takes is the struggle over the rate of exploitation - how much workers get to keep of what they produce.

In the last third of the 18th century, workers' resistance to long working hours in England's factories forced the government to pass **legislation** limiting and regulating the working day. With capitalists trying to extend the length of the working day as far as possible and workers trying to reduce it, the actual length of the working day is decided by class struggle between capitalists and workers where 'force decides'.

Mainstream economists and politicians use the word exploitation to refer to particularly bad pay or working conditions as if the general relationship between the capitalist class and the working class is not exploitative. The explanation of the origins of surplus value in *Capital* shows how exploitation is not something that particularly greedy capitalists do but something all capitalists do because it is what capitalism exists to do.

4 Productivity

Surplus value produced by lengthening the working day beyond necessary labour time is called **absolute surplus value**.

The only way capitalists can increase the amount of surplus labour time in a working day, and therefore increase surplus value, without lengthening the working day is by increasing the productivity of labour so that commodities become cheaper and less labour time is needed to produce the workers' means of subsistence. This reduces the value of labour power and therefore necessary labour time, allowing surplus labour time to lengthen without lengthening the working day. Surplus value produced by increasing productivity is called **relative surplus value**.

If a capitalist doubles productivity, twice as many products are made each day and the value of each produced commodity halves. Why would any capitalist want to reduce the value of the commodities they produce? The answer lies in the difference between the **individual value** of a commodity, the labour time it takes a particular producer to produce it, and its actual, social value, the labour time socially necessary to produce it.

Imagine a table takes 20 hours to produce and sells at a direct price of £20. If one table-making capitalist improves productivity so that their workers can make a table in 15 hours, its individual value for that capitalist will be £15, £5 under the direct price of £20.

Our capitalist can make £5 more surplus value on each table their workers produce by selling them for £20. Alternatively, our capitalist could sell more tables by reducing their price to above their individual value but under its direct price, say £17, squeezing an extra surplus value of £2 out of each table while still undercutting competing capitalists.

It is this extra surplus value, the difference between the amount of labour it normally takes to make a commodity and the amount of labour an innovating capitalist needs to make it, that gives every capitalist an interest in increasing productivity and cheapening the commodities they produce.

Once they have done this, other capitalists are forced to increase their own productivity to match our innovative capitalist or lose sales. Once this happens the extra surplus value our innovating capitalist has been making disappears. The value of tables is reduced from 20 hours of socially necessary abstract labour to 15 hours and its direct price falls from £20 to £15.

The extra surplus value temporarily gained by the innovating capitalist is not relative surplus value. Individual capitalists cannot produce relative surplus value on their own.

Relative surplus value is produced when increased productivity reduces the time taken to produce the worker's means of subsistence and so increases surplus labour time and surplus value. This means improving productivity in the branches of industry that produce means of subsistence for workers or the means of production for producing these means of subsistence.

Increases in productivity in industries making **luxuries** that are only consumed by capitalists do not reduce the value of labour power and so do not produce relative surplus value.

While an individual capitalist increasing productivity gains extra surplus value for a time, increasing productivity reduces surplus value for capital as a whole. Less labour goes into each commodity resulting in each commodity having less value.

We will look at the implications of this contradiction between capital's drive to increase productivity and its drive to expand surplus value in *Part 14 The falling rate of profit*. For now we investigate how capital increases productivity and the effects this increase has on society and nature.

The first way capital reorganises the labour process to increase productivity is by merging medieval workshops into large workplaces where a large group of workers produce commodities under the control of a single capitalist. This **cooperation** between large numbers of workers in the labour process 'forms the starting-point of capitalist production'.

Even without any other change in the labour process, bringing workers together to produce commodities saves capitalists money by spreading costs of means of production such as energy and space over more produced commodities.

As cooperation develops, the labour process takes on a continuity and uniformity that forces workers to labour at a consistent pace. Timekeeping by clock measures the time it takes to produce a specific amount of commodities more accurately so it can be reduced to a minimum.

Each individual worker is different, but once a large number of workers are employed together each individual worker's working day forms a part of the **collective working day** which, if divided by the number of workers, gives one day of **average social labour**. The **collective labour** of the **collective worker** produces a greater quantity of use values than workers labouring individually for the same amount of working days, reducing the labour time needed to produce a certain amount of use values.

The extra productivity that results from collective labour is the **productive power of social labour.** This productive power is a free gift to capital which capital is always developing to make more productive use of labour power.

In any society, the labour process must be organised. In capitalism, the labour process is also a process to create as much surplus value as possible by exploiting workers. Cooperation under the direction of a capitalist makes the subjection of labour to capital central to the labour process. Capitalists have to pay out some variable capital to employ a special kind of worker as **supervisors,** a necessary cost to discipline the workforce into maximising production and deal with any workers' resistance to their exploitation.

Workers own their labour power until they sell it to the capitalist, when it becomes capital in the labour process. As the cooperation of workers is brought about by the capitalist who employs them and controls the labour process, the productive power of social labour appears to be the **productive power of capital** and capitalists appear to be the wealth creators rather than workers.

As cooperation grows so does the **division of labour in production**. Skilled handicrafts are split up into series of small operations each carried out by a particular group of workers. While the division of labour in society disperses the means of production among many capitalists with no one in overall charge, the division of labour in production centralises the means of production under the control of individual capitalists.

'Anarchy in the social division of labour and despotism in that of the workshop are mutual conditions the one of the other'.

The production of commodities on a large scale using cooperation and division of labour in the labour process is called **manufacture**. During the manufacturing period from the mid 16th to the late 18th century, manufacture transformed the labour process, increasing its speed and intensity and 'riveting each labourer to a single fractional detail' to create 'a productive mechanism whose parts are human beings'.

The growth of manufacture in Britain and some other European countries was dependent on the creation of a worldwide system of **colonialism** based on the exploitation of labour and the theft of natural resources from colonised countries for use as raw materials for manufacture. Without the fruits of this theft, manufacture could not have developed in the early capitalist countries of Europe.

The industrial revolution of the 18th century transformed manufacture into modern **industry** by expanding the use of **machines** in the labour process. Machines increase productivity by replacing skilled workers operating tools with machines able to operate more tools quicker, producing more use values from the same amount of labour.

The **productive power of machines** is measured by how much they increase the productivity of labour. A machine that replaces ten workers and lasts for ten years has twice the productive power of a machine that only replaces five workers and lasts for ten years or a machine that still replaces ten workers but only lasts for five years. The more workers a machine replaces, and the longer it replaces them for, the more productive power it has.

Unlike cooperation or the division of labour, capitalists have to pay for machines. Capitalists will only buy machines if they cost less than the labour power they replace. Machines gradually lose their value through wear and tear in the labour process, their use value and therefore the value needed to reproduce them diminishing over time. This transfer of the value of the machine to produced commodities through wear and tear is called **physical depreciation**.

Wear and tear is not the only way that machines lose their value. The value of a machine, like the value of any commodity, is determined by the amount of labour it takes to reproduce it at a particular time rather than the amount of labour it took to produce it originally.

Increasing productivity means machines are constantly being replaced by better, cheaper machines, reducing the value of older machines even if they are working perfectly well. The older machine undergoes **moral depreciation** and so transfers less value to the product, despite no change in the labour process involving the old machine.

Capitalists find themselves having to replace machines long before they are physically worn out because of moral depreciation. In anticipation of this, capitalists try to shorten the time taken to reproduce a machine's value by lengthening the working day. As the natural and social limits to the length of the working day assert themselves, capitalists intensify the labour carried out during these limited hours by increasing the speed machines run at and making workers operate larger and more machines.

Machines need an **energy source** other than human labour to power them. Horse power was unreliable and costly, and not easily applicable in factories. Wind power was 'too inconstant and uncontrollable, and besides, in England, the birthplace of modern industry, the use of water power preponderated even during the manufacturing period'. Water power could be used to create energy, but as a source of energy water 'could not be increased at will, it failed at certain seasons of the year, and, above all, it was essentially local'.

The steam engine, using coal to produce steam, was a much more reliable source of energy for powering machines than wind or water. 'No system of machinery could be properly developed before the steam-engine' because steam allowed capitalists to expand production by concentrating masses of workers in factories in towns.

The steam engine 'did not give rise to any industrial revolution. It was, on the contrary, the invention of machines that made a revolution in the form of steam-engines necessary'.

The extraction of carbon from nature for use as fossil fuel on an ever-expanding scale became an essential part of industry. Energy from carbon stored in nature as fossil fuel allowed industry to make the product of past labours contribute to the labour process on a large scale for the first time by the production of machines, stored dead labour that increases the productivity of the labour process.

The industrial labour process is carried out in **factories**, places where machines dominate production in 'an organised system of machines, a mechanical monster whose body fills whole factories' that is able to transform raw materials into commodities with little human labour other than for supervision and repair.

As production expands, a **division of labour by region** develops with different **branches of industry** concentrated in different geographical areas. With carbon as an energy source, the need for labour power to have physical strength is replaced by a need for dexterity and skills. This results in women and children being employed more as workers, expanding the number of workers in each household, reducing the value of each worker's labour power.

Machines increase the rapidity and intensity of the labour process, forcing workers to adapt to their rhythms so that instead of the worker consuming the material elements of his productive activity, 'they consume him'. Manufacture's cooperation and division of labour between workers is replaced by industry's cooperation and division of labour between an organised system of machines that form a **collective machine** supervised by workers.

'By means of its conversion into an automaton, the instrument of labour confronts the labourer, during the labour-process, in the shape of capital, of dead labour, that dominates, and pumps dry, living labour-power. The separation of the intellectual powers of production from the **manual labour,** and the conversion of those powers into the might of capital over labour, is, as we have already seen, finally completed by modern industry erected on the foundation of machinery.'

The use of machines in one industry requires the use of machines in others. In contrast to earlier modes of production, capital's drive to create surplus value without limit means that it 'never looks upon and treats the existing form of a process as final'. There is an increased demand for labour for large projects like canals, docks, tunnels and bridges that need large amounts of capital to be invested that will only bear fruit years in the future. Means of communication and transport speed up and expand production by developing new connections across the world.

As machines develop and the amount and variety of commodities being produced expand, the constant development of the labour process creates a need for an adaptable workforce. The separation of manual labour from the design and control of the labour process, and the need for a **scientific** understanding of the labour process so that ever more efficient machines can be created, leads some workers to carry out **universal labour**, a form of **intellectual labour** that adds to human knowledge with the aim of developing science and **technology**. The **productive power of science** becomes a productive force distinct from the labour that directly produces commodities.

The large scale use of machines in capitalist countries allows them to produce commodities much cheaper than in countries where production is dominated by handicraft. 'A new and **international division of labour** suited to the requirements of the chief centres of modern industry springs up, and converts one part of the globe into a chiefly agricultural field of production, for supplying the other part which remains a chiefly industrial field'.

'By ruining handicraft production in other countries, machinery forcibly converts them into fields for the supply of its raw material. In this way East India was compelled to produce cotton, wool, hemp, jute, and indigo for Great Britain'.

On the one hand, the extraordinary rise in productivity allows a growing part of production to be devoted to producing luxuries for personal consumption by whoever can afford them. On the other hand, capital's obsessional need to maximise surplus value drives capitalists to increase the exploitation of workers beyond what is reasonable for human beings, endangering workers' safety and exposing them to life-threatening environments. As far as workers' conditions are concerned 'the capitalist mode of production, owing to its very nature, excludes all rational improvement beyond a certain point'.

Just as capitalist production increases the productivity of labour to maximise surplus value without any concern for the wellbeing of workers, it exploits the **productive power of nature** to increase productivity without any concern for the sustainability of nature as the source of that productive power.

Capitalist production 'develops technology, and the combining together of various processes into a social whole, only by sapping the original sources of all wealth - the soil and the labourer'.

'All progress in capitalistic agriculture is a progress in the art, not only of robbing the labourer, but of robbing the soil; all progress in increasing the fertility of the soil for a given time, is a progress towards ruining the lasting sources of that fertility'.

'Capitalist production, by collecting the population in great centres, and causing an ever-increasing preponderance of town population, on the one hand concentrates the historical motive power of society; on the other hand, it disturbs the **circulation of matter** between man and the soil, i.e., prevents the return to the soil of its elements consumed by man in the form of food and clothing; it therefore violates the conditions necessary to lasting fertility of the soil'.

'Capitalist production completely tears asunder the old bond of union which held together agriculture and manufacture in their infancy. But at the same time it creates the material conditions for a higher synthesis in the future, viz., the union of agriculture and industry on the basis of the more perfected forms they have each acquired during their temporary separation', restoring the circulation of matter 'as a regulating law of social production, and under a form appropriate to the full development of the human race'.

Capital has developed the world's productive forces to a level at which all human needs can easily be met in a sustainable way.[1] Cooperation in the labour process, the division of labour, the use of machinery, the development of technology and the centralisation of production have created labour processes where workers carry out most of the world's commodity production in a highly organised way, islands of planned production in a sea of competing capitals.

The use values capital produces are irrelevant to it. Capital wants to sell as many commodities as possible because every commodity produced contains surplus value. Capitalists create new addictions and wants through advertising, marketing, branding and so on in order to produce and sell more, with no concern for the impact this production has on nature, workers or consumers.

Capital's drive to expand and increase productivity increases the amount of use values labour produces as ever more labour, natural resources and energy are turned into new commodities with the sole aim of producing surplus value for capitalists.

This has dramatically increased the impact humans have on the rest of nature. The total weight of everything humans extract from nature to consume in a year rose from 7 billion tons in 1900 to 14 billion tons in 1950 and 92 billion tons in 2017.[2]

This weight is not evenly distributed. When it comes to emissions of greenhouse gases, the average person in a high income country emits more than 30 times that of someone in a low income country.[3]

Capital's impact on nature has now reached the level where we have entered the **anthropocene**, or capitalocene as some call it, a geological age where human activity has a significant impact on our planetary ecological systems.[4]

A rational society run by associated producers would abolish capital and shift production from maximising surplus value to meeting personal, social and ecological needs. Humans would collectively organise their relationship with the rest of nature in a conscious manner that meets people's needs in a sustainable way while repairing the damage caused by capital.

The abolition of pointless production in a socialist society would reduce the working day, creating more free time for meeting social needs and personal and social development. Science and technology would continue to develop, creating new ways of producing use values with less labour and and no ecological damage. Production would be transformed from being a way for one class to exploit another class into an expression of human creativity.

We saw in *Part 3 Exploitation* how capital's inexorable

extension of the working day led to struggles to limit it. Just as the fight for a shorter working day has always been a key part of the fight against capital, the struggle to limit capital's destruction of ecologies, from the extraction of fossil fuel to the cutting down of rain forests, is a key part of the fight against capital today.

5 Subsumption

Cooperation and the division of labour create workforces where different workers taking on different tasks in the labour process form a collective worker producing commodities. As labour processes develop and new types of commodities are produced, new types of manual and intellectual labour are needed too. Any worker contributing to the development or production of commodities that produces surplus value for a capitalist is a **productive worker** doing **productive labour**.

A commodity does not have to be a physical object for the labour producing it to be productive. Capitalists can employs workers to provide **services**, commodities consumed at the same time as they are produced, as when a musician plays a concert or a bus driver takes passengers to their destination.

A worker who does not produce surplus value, for instance a personal servant or a state employed nurse, is an **unproductive worker** carrying out **unproductive labour**. The same kind of concrete labour can be either productive or not productive of capital. 'A schoolmaster is a productive labourer when, in addition to belabouring the heads of his scholars, he works like a horse to enrich the school proprietor. That the latter has laid out his capital in a teaching factory, instead of in a sausage factory, does not alter the relation'. We will see in *Part 9 Circulation* how capital needs some kinds of unproductive labour as much as it needs productive labour if it is to reproduce itself and expand.

The production of a surplus in any society is only possible because humans are able to produce more use values than they need to survive. The extent to which this happens depends on physical conditions such as the fertility of the soil, the climate and the availability of raw materials. The more favourable the natural environment a society exists in, the smaller the necessary labour time of the working population and the more labour can be surplus labour.

But a fertile environment does not impose the necessity of developing productivity and using **free time** to produce more than is needed. It is in climates where more labour is needed to survive that capitalist production 'based on the dominion of man over nature' begins its growth. 'It is the necessity of bringing a natural force under the control of society, of economising, of appropriating or subduing it on a large scale by the work of man's hand, that first plays the decisive part in the history of industry'.

Someone living in a fertile environment where they only have to work one day a week to satisfy their wants has been given a lot of free time by nature. Once capitalist production imposes itself, the same person might have to work five days a week to earn enough wages to satisfy the same wants as they previously satisfied by working for one day because as a wage worker they have to perform surplus labour for a capitalist as well as necessary labour. Nature explains why they only needed to work one day for themselves, but only capital's need to produce surplus value explains the five days. Capital always seeks to increase the amount of surplus labour performed by workers. 'In capitalist society spare time is acquired for one class by converting the whole life-time of the masses into labour time'.

Capital creates the conditions for its own expansion through the **subsumption** of other ways of making products, turning production of products for use and exchange with other producers into production of commodities by workers for capitalists. This process is called the **formal subsumption** of labour under capital, capital taking hold of a given labour process and using it to create surplus value, with the labour process directed by a capitalist, a capitalist owning the product and the individual worker paid in wages.

Some production is carried out by the **intermediate subsumption** of labour under capital, where capital does not control the labour process or pay wages but buys products made by independent producers outside the circuit of capital. Capital exploits this labour by paying producers less than the value of their products.

As cooperation and the division of labour under the control of individual capitalists expands, the formal subsumption of labour to capital is replaced by the **real subsumption** of labour under capital. Machines introduced by capitalists take control of production, allowing increased productivity of labour and the production of relative surplus value.

The amount of machines, factories and infrastructure containing dead labour increases enormously. Living labour becomes controlled by the needs and rhythms of the factory, with machines controlling workers rather than workers controlling machines.

As a result of commodity fetishism, the products of human labour appear to be products of the productive power of capital itself. Capital becomes synonymous with the means of production as if capital is made up of things rather than relationships between people.

As productivity increases, the value of workers' means of subsistence falls. It becomes quite possible for the amount of means of subsistence to keep growing and for workers' standards of living to keep rising as the value of these means of subsistence falls.

'But even in such case, the fall in the value of labour-power would cause a corresponding rise of surplus-value, and thus the abyss between the labourer's position and that of the capitalist would keep widening'.

6 Wages

A **wage** is the price a capitalist pays a worker for the use of their labour power during the working day. The value of any commodity is the value of the commodities needed to reproduce it, so the value of labour power is the worker's means of subsistence.

As we saw in *Part 3 Exploitation*, the value that a worker's labour power produces in a day is greater than the value of their labour power. Workers produce the value of their labour power plus the surplus value that capitalists take from them.

But this is not how things appear. Wages seem to be payment for all the labour the worker performs, not just part of it. Wages hide the exploitation of workers, extinguishing 'every trace of the division of the working-day into necessary labour and surplus-labour, into paid and unpaid labour. All labour appears as paid labour'.

The appearance of exploitation as a "a fair day's work for a fair day's pay" 'forms the basis of all the juridical notions of both labourer and capitalist, of all the mystifications of the capitalistic mode of production, of all its illusions as to liberty'.

Like the price of other commodities, wages fluctuate

around the value of the commodity, in this case the value of labour power. Capitalists try to reduce workers' wages without reducing the surplus value workers produce by reducing the amount of necessary labour time and increasing the amount of surplus labour time. If a capitalist is able to increase the length of the working day without increasing wages, the capitalist can extract more surplus value.

As productivity increases, the price of the means of subsistence falls, lowering the **nominal wage**, the amount of money in the wage, needed to buy a particular amount of commodities, the **real wage**. This allows capitalists to increase the rate of exploitation without lowering workers' standard of living.

Workers paid **time wages** are paid for the amount of time they labour. In some branches of industry the working day is paid at a certain rate up to a certain point beyond which workers do **overtime**. In some industries overtime is expected but not paid, an extension of surplus labour time, in others it is paid at a higher rate.

Paid overtime always produces more value for capitalists than the extra wages paid - they wouldn't offer it if it didn't - allowing capitalists to make more use of machines and other means of production, sometimes with shift work and 24 hour production.

Low wages for normal hours often compel workers to work overtime if they are to earn a living wage, lengthening the working day. As low paid workers have to work longer to earn even an average wage 'it is a fact generally known that the longer the working day in a branch of industry, the lower are the wages'.

When capitalists impose **casualisation** on a labour process, the working day stops containing a definite number of hours and capitalists can wring surplus labour from workers without allowing them the labour time necessary for their own subsistence. Capitalists stop paying workers for any hours they are not needed and shifts become irregular, allowing the capitalist to 'make the most enormous overwork alternate with relative or absolute cessation of work'. The casualisation of labour also makes it more difficult for workers to raise wages and improve conditions collectively.

Capitalists sometimes pay workers for the amount of commodities they produce rather than for the hours they labour. These **piece wages** are a converted form of time wages where less supervision is needed to ensure the intensity of labour because workers have an interest in producing as many commodities as they can.

The value of labour power, and therefore wage levels, are different in different countries depending on the level of productivity, 'the price and the extent of the prime necessaries of life as naturally and historically developed' and other factors. Countries with higher productivity tend to have higher real wages because they produce more commodities with the same amount of labour.

We saw in *Part 4 Productivity* that more productive labour processes need less labour to produce commodities than the average labour process so the commodities they produce have an individual value below the average, social value.

On the world market, countries with higher productivity than other countries need less labour to produce commodities giving their commodities a **national value** below the average **international value** of the commodity. A commodity that takes an hour of labour to produce in a more productive country might take ten or a hundred hours of labour to produce in a less productive country.

'So long as the more productive nation is not compelled by competition to lower the selling price of its commodities to the level of their value', 'the different quantities of commodities of the same kind, produced in different countries in the same working-time, have, therefore, unequal international values, which are expressed in different prices'.

We will see how this **unequal exchange** of labour between capitalists in countries with different levels of productivity helps maintain the division of the world into rich and poor countries in *Part 13 Competition.*

7 Accumulation

Capitalist production not only produces commodities and surplus value, it also reproduces the **capitalist relationship** of wage worker to capitalist, labour to capital. As we saw in *Part 2 Capital and labour power*, capital has to expand. It can only expand by consuming labour, by workers selling their alienated labour power to capitalists in return for wages. Capital's self-expansion and the exploitative relationship between worker and capitalist are the same thing.

Once labour power becomes a commodity and the capitalist relationship is established as the main relationship of production, the **formal equality** between commodity producers exchanging commodities of equal value with each other becomes its opposite, exploitation and inequality between the owners of the means of production and workers. As we saw in *Part 6 Wages*, the payment of wages in return for labour power, an exchange of commodities of equal value, hides the exploitative nature of capitalist production.

'A society can no more cease to produce than it can cease to consume. When viewed, therefore, as a connected whole, and as flowing on with incessant renewal, every social process of production is, at the same time, a process of reproduction'. Although this **reproduction of capital** 'is a mere repetition of the process of production on the old scale, yet this mere repetition, or continuity, gives a new character to the process'.

Capital is the surplus labour of workers transformed into an alien power that dominates and exploits them in order to expand itself. 'Since the process of production is also the process by which the capitalist consumes labour power, the product of the labourer is incessantly converted, not only into commodities, but into capital, into value that sucks up the value-creating power, into means of subsistence that buy the person of the labourer, into means of production that command the producers'.

Capitalist production involves two types of consumption by workers, the **productive consumption** of the means of production by their labour in the labour process in order to produce new value for capitalists and the **individual consumption** of their means of subsistence outside the labour process in order to live.

The individual consumption of workers is as necessary to the capitalist as their productive consumption. The worker's individual consumption allows the means of subsistence to be turned into new labour power at the disposal of capital for exploitation. 'It is the production and reproduction of that means of production so indispensable to the capitalist: the labourer himself'. While capitalist production expands capital for the capitalist, it leaves the worker 'what he was on entering it, a source of wealth, but devoid of all means of making that wealth his own'.

In the labour process workers produce commodities equal to the value of the wages they receive to buy the consumer goods that make up their means of subsistence plus the surplus value taken by capitalists. This surplus value is either consumed by capitalists as **revenue** that buys the consumer goods that make up their means of subsistence and luxuries they consume individually or it is reinvested as capital.

If we assume that all surplus value is consumed individually by capitalists and none reinvested as capital, then **simple reproduction** of capital would take place. But capital cannot simply reproduce itself without growing, as competition compels capitalists to constantly extend their capital in order to preserve it. For the capitalist, 'so far as he is personified capital, it is not values in use and the enjoyment of them, but exchange-value and its augmentation, that spur him into action'. The accumulation of capital is the subjective aim of the capitalist. 'To accumulate, is to conquer the world of social wealth, to increase the mass of human beings exploited by him, and thus to extend both the direct and the indirect sway of the capitalist'.

The **accumulation of capital** is the conversion of surplus value into capital and therefore 'the reproduction of capital on a progressively increasing scale'. In place of the circular movement implied by the simple reproduction of capital, the real movement of capital is a spiral, constantly expanding by absorbing surplus value produced by workers, a constant increase in production driven by the self-expansion of capital.

In any society, production involves a definite quantity of living labour consuming the free gifts of nature and a definite quantity of dead labour contained in the means of production. In capitalist production, the ratio between the amount of living labour and dead labour employed in the labour process is called the **technical composition of capital**. A labour process where a hundred workers make a hundred tables a day with a few simple tools has a lower technical composition than a process where ten workers make a hundred tables a day using cooperation, the division of labour and machinery.

As productivity increases and the technical composition of capital rises, this is reflected in a rise in the **value composition of capital**, the ratio between the value of constant capital and variable capital. 'Between the two there is a strict correlation'. The value composition of capital tends to rise, but not as fast as the technical composition because, as a result of growing productivity, the value of constant capital and labour power keeps falling.

If wages rise or fall, or the cost of means of production changes, the value composition of the capital changes without changing the technical composition of capital. Insofar as the value composition of capital is determined by its technical composition it is called the **organic composition of capital**. Increasing productivity, competition, workers' struggles and the progress of science and technology means that the organic composition of capital tends to rise over time as the productive power of social labour increases.

Accumulation leads to the **centralisation of capital**, the transformation of lots of small capitals into fewer large ones. Centralisation intensifies and accelerates the rise in the organic composition of capital as larger capitals are able to concentrate and expand labour processes. 'The masses of capital fused together overnight by centralisation which reproduce and multiply... becoming new and powerful levers in social accumulation'.

Once we bring increasing productivity and the accumulation of capital into our investigation, the law of value implies the **law of capitalist accumulation** that as capital accumulates and centralises, the organic composition of capital rises and living labour is replaced by machines, reducing the amount of living labour needed to produce commodities. This process creates a **relative surplus population** that becomes a 'condition of existence of the capitalist mode of production'. This relative surplus population of unemployed workers able to replace workers if they complain too much is 'the pivot upon which the law of demand and supply of labour works. It confines the field of action of this law within the limits absolutely convenient to the activity of exploitation and to the domination of capital'.

Instead of material wealth being used to satisfy the needs of its producers, capital only employs workers to expand capital. Instead of greater productivity increasing wealth for everyone, the greater the productivity of labour the more capitalists accumulate and the more precarious workers' lives become. Exploitation is intensified rather than abolished and 'all means for the development of production transform themselves into means of domination over, and exploitation of, the producers'.

The relative surplus population is composed of different layers. The **floating surplus population** consists of workers who move in and out of work and who are currently unemployed. Part of this floating surplus population follows exported capital and emigrates. The **latent surplus population** consists of people not yet fully integrated into capitalist production, such as peasants and agricultural workers, who are often forced by poverty in the countryside to move to cities to find work. The

stagnant surplus population consists of casual workers with extremely irregular employment, low pay and dangerous working conditions. Lastly, a **destitute surplus population** living in extreme poverty just below the rest of the surplus population becomes 'a condition of capitalist production, and of the capitalist development of wealth'. While capital condemns millions to destitution, 'capital knows how to throw these, for the most part, from its own shoulders on to those of the working class and the lower middle class'.

Wages become regulated by the expansion and contraction of a disposable **reserve army of labour** within the relative surplus population that forces workers 'to submit to overwork and to subjugation under the dictates of capital'.

'Accumulation of wealth at one pole is, therefore, at the same time accumulation of misery, agony of toil, slavery, ignorance, brutality, mental degradation, at the opposite pole *i.e.*, on the side of the class that produces its own product in the form of capital.'

The expansions and contractions of the industrial reserve army settle into an **industrial cycle** where accumulation leads to a **boom** in production, employment and wages followed by a crisis when production crashes followed by a period of **recession** leading to a **recovery** which creates a new boom.

Capitalist accumulation has seen the global economy grow from being worth about $1 trillion in today's money in the 19th century to over $80 trillion today.[1] As capital has accumulated, its growth has accelerated so that between 1700 and 1870 world production increased by 200%, between 1870 and 1940 it increased by 300% and between 1940 and 2015 it increased by 1,300%.[2]

The centralisation of capital has led to a few large companies dominating most branches of industry. 17 companies manage half the production on the planet.[3] Four companies control 90% of global grain supply.[4]

The concentration of wealth that capitalism creates is reflected in grotesque inequality between individuals. 1% of the world's adults own nearly half of all personal wealth while the poorest half of the world's population own around 1%.[5] This inequality in wealth keeps growing, as nearly twice as much of the wealth produced by workers goes to the richest 1% than to the rest of the world's population.[6]

8 Origins

Although capitalist production existed sporadically in some Mediterranean towns as early as the 14th century, the era of capitalist production dates from the 16th century. Before this, the dominant **mode of production** in England, which we take as our example because it was the country where capitalist production first became established, was **feudalism** where most people were **peasants** in servitude to a feudal **landowner**. Peasants worked a piece of land while paying rent in the form of goods or labour to the landowner.

Peasant families were largely self-sufficient, producing and consuming most of what they needed with their own labour through a mixture of working the land and **domestic industry**. Peasant families owned their own means of production in a system of **individual private property** and **individual production**.

'In themselves money and commodities are no more capital than are the means of production and of subsistence'. For these things to become capital 'two very different kinds of commodity-possessors must come face to face and into contact; on the one hand, the owners of money, means of production, means of subsistence, who are eager to increase the sum of values they possess, by buying other people's labour power; on the other hand, free labourers, the sellers of their own labour power, and therefore the sellers of labour' 'unencumbered by any means of production of their own'.

'The process, therefore, that clears the way for the capitalist system, can be none other than the process which takes away from the labourer the possession of his means of production; a process that transforms, on the one hand, the social means of subsistence and of production into capital, on the other, the immediate producers into wage labourers'. This primitive or **original accumulation** of capital 'is nothing else than the historical process of divorcing the producer from the means of production', a process of **enclosure** and **expropriation** of the land 'written in the annals of mankind in letters of blood and fire'.

The expulsion of the mass of the population from the land forced peasants and rural workers to move to towns and cities to sell their labour power as a commodity to industrial capitalists in return for wages. This established the capitalist relationship between capitalist and wage worker as the dominant relationship of production and capitalism as the dominant mode of production.

The original accumulation of capital saw the replacement of domestic industry and small **guild** workshops by capitalist factories where cooperation and the division of labour transformed the labour process and started the expansion of production described in *Part 4 Productivity*. The transformation of feudal exploitation into capitalist exploitation did nothing to change the fact that a small number of exploiters lived off the labour of the majority.

With most of the agricultural population forced off the land, domestic industry in the countryside was destroyed as farmers started to buy cheaper goods made in the factories of industrial capitalists rather than the more expensive products of domestic industry. The division between private, domestic labour carried out mainly by women to reproduce labour power at home and wage labour carried out by wage workers for capitalists in factories became established.

The expulsion of peasants from the land resulted in 'the forcible creation of a class of outlawed proletarians' robbed of their means of production but unable to find employment with the early industrial capitalists. Many of these unemployed workers were forced into destitution to be faced with 'a bloody legislation against vagabondage'.

'Thus were the agricultural people, first forcibly expropriated from the soil, driven from their homes, turned into vagabonds, and then whipped, branded, tortured by laws grotesquely terrible, into the discipline necessary for the wage system', becoming the first reserve army of labour.

Capitalists used the power of the state, the 'concentrated and organised force of society', to crush resistance to enforced enclosure, impose wage limits on workers and 'employed the police to accelerate the accumulation of capital by increasing the degree of exploitation of labour'.

This ensured the constant generation of a relative surplus population that kept wages low enough to allow the production of surplus value. Once the capitalist relationship of workers selling their labour power to capitalists in return for wages was established 'the dull compulsion of economic relations completes the subjection of the labourer to the capitalist'.

Enclosures and expropriations left a few rich landowners owning the land previously worked by peasants. These landowners rented land to richer former peasants who had become **capitalist farmers** by hiring **agricultural workers** to work the land in return for wages. The production and consumption of the means of subsistence within rural communities was replaced by agricultural workers producing commodities worth more than their means of subsistence for capitalist farmers in return for their means of subsistence in the form of wages.

The concentration of means of production in the hands of capitalist farmers raised the productivity of agriculture, allowing more use values to be produced than before with less labour. By the end of the 16th century England had a class of capitalist farmers, 'rich, considering the circumstances of the time'.

As feudal society dissolved, some guild-masters, artisans and others were able to transform themselves into capitalists. Some **usurers** and **merchants** were able to transform their **usurers' capital**, based on lending money and receiving more back, and **merchants' capital**, based on buying cheap and selling dear, into industrial capital.

However, 'the snail's pace of this method corresponded in no wise with the commercial requirements of the new world market that the great discoveries of the end of the 15th century created'. The accumulation of capital in early capitalist countries like England and Holland was only possible because of colonialism, the theft of resources and labour from conquered countries for use as capital in a few rich countries.

'The treasures captured outside Europe by undisguised looting, enslavement, and murder, floated back to the mother-country and were there turned into capital'. The discovery of gold and silver in America, the conquest and looting of much of the world and 'the turning of Africa into a warren for the commercial hunting of black-skins' formed the basis of capital's original accumulation.

'Whilst the cotton industry introduced child-slavery in England, it gave in the United States a stimulus to the transformation of the earlier, more or less patriarchal **slavery**, into a system of commercial exploitation'. 'The veiled slavery of the wage workers in Europe needed, for its pedestal, slavery pure and simple in the new world'.

Colonialism not only provided the raw materials manufacture needed, it also created a market for early manufacture, and, through the **monopoly** of markets by colonialist countries, an increasing accumulation of capital. Competing capitalist countries carried out **protectionism** to increase their own country's capital at the expense of others, charging duties and taxes to protect their interests, leading to 'the **commercial war** of the European nations, with the globe for a theatre'.

By the end of the 17th century England had a system of colonialism and protectionism financed by a **national debt**. The system of national debt had its origins in Genoa and Venice as early as the middle ages but only took possession of Europe during the manufacturing period. 'The colonial system with its maritime trade and commercial wars served as a forcing-house for it'.

The system of national debt works by the state borrowing money from **banks**. These banks 'decorated with national titles' were originally groups of private speculators who used their connections with governments to lend money to the state. The banks gave nothing away as in return for their loans they received easily negotiable **bonds**.

The national debt can be measured by 'the successive rise in the stock of these banks, whose full development dates from the founding of the Bank of England in 1694. The Bank of England began by lending its money to the government at 8% at the same time as it was empowered by Parliament to lend the same capital to the public in the form of banknotes'. Soon these banknotes became the form in which 'the Bank of England made its loans to the state, and paid, on account of the state, the interest on the public debt'.

This process allowed the Bank of England to become 'the eternal creditor of the nation' holding the national gold reserve and the centre of gravity of all commercial credit. The national debt became crucial to original accumulation by endowing 'barren money with the power of breeding' as it became capital.

In order to pay the interest on the national debt to the banks, the state raised funds through **taxation** 'on the most necessary means of subsistence'. 'The only part of the so-called national wealth that actually enters into the collective possessions of modern peoples is their national debt'.

Capital expands and centralises production, increasing the productivity of the labour process through the application of technology and science, socialising labour and creating the world market. 'Along with the constantly diminishing number of the magnates of capital, who usurp and monopolise all advantages of this process of transformation, grows the mass of misery, oppression, slavery, degradation, exploitation.'

In the colonies 'the capitalist regime everywhere comes into collision with the resistance of the producer, who, as owner of his own conditions of labour, employs that labour to enrich himself, instead of the capitalist'. 'The contradiction of these two diametrically opposed economic systems, manifests itself here practically in a struggle between them'.

In capitalist societies, individual production based on individual private property is transformed into capitalist production based on **capitalist private property** where capitalists owning the means of production expand their wealth through cooperation, the division of labour, the concentration of production and the centralisation of the ownership of capital.

The transition from feudalism to capitalism came about when the growing **forces of production** developed during feudalism outgrew feudalism's **relations of production** that stopped productivity increasing. Class struggle by capitalists allowed them to expand capitalist production in a way that put an end to most feudal relations of production - but not all, as we will see in *Part 17 Rent*.

Today, the forces of production that capitalism has developed through its need to increase productivity have outgrown the capitalist relationship. Production has developed worldwide to the extent that it could easily meet the needs of everyone in the world. However capitalist relations of production prevent these forces of production from doing this because the means of production are in the hands of a few capitalists solely concerned with increasing surplus value.

This contradiction leads to class struggle between workers and capitalists where workers demand that society be organised in their interests. This can only be done on the basis of **collective production** where the means of production are the **collective property** of a classless society of associated producers based on 'cooperation and the possession in common of the land and of the means of production'.

9 Circulation

In parts 9, 10 and 11, the second volume of *Capital*, we investigate how capital circulates and reproduces itself.

In *Part 2 Capital and labour power* we saw that the general formula for capital in circulation is M-C-M', money buying commodities that are used to produce new commodities with a higher value than the commodities bought to make them. We now look further into this circuit as it applies to **industrial capital**, the capital involving capitalist production that we have been examining up till now, as distinct from capital that does not involve production that we will examine in *Part 15 Commerce* and *Part 16 Interest and fictitious capital*.

In the **circuit of industrial capital**, capital continually changes its form from **money capital** into **productive capital** then **commodity capital** then money capital again. Capital moves between private **spheres of production** where productive capital produces commodity capital and the public **sphere of circulation** where capitalists use money capital to buy commodity capital for use in production and sell the commodity capital their workers produce, **realising** the value in the produced commodity capital by turning it into money capital.

The circuit of industrial capital is put into motion when an **industrial capitalist** with money (M) buys two kinds of commodity capital (C), labour power (L) and means of production (MP), with the purpose of making more money. The productive consumption of the means of production by labour during the labour process (P) produces new commodities (C') with more value than the labour and means of production used up in their production. The capitalist then sells these commodities for more money (M') than they advanced. Using lines to indicate exchange and dots to indicate an interruption in the circulation process, the formula for the circuit of industrial capital can be written as

$$M-C \ (L + MP) \ ... \ P \ ... \ C'-M'$$

For capital to complete this circuit a lot of conditions need to be met. Assuming no trade with non-capitalist economies,

- for capitalists to buy labour power (M-L) they must be able to find workers willing and able to sell their labour power in exchange for the wages they offer
- for labour power to be reproduced, unpaid domestic labour must reproduce the worker
- for workers to buy their means of subsistence there must be capitalists selling them at prices workers can afford
- for capitalists to buy means of production (M-MP) there must be other capitalists selling them at prices that allow them to make surplus value
- for capitalist production (P) to take place, labour power and the means of production must be used to create new commodity capital (C') and surplus value

- for capitalists to sell the commodities they produce (C'-M') there must be workers and other capitalists with enough money to buy them
- for capitalists to spend some of the surplus value contained in M' as revenue for individual consumption of luxuries someone must be producing these luxuries.

Every capitalist wants their capital to circulate as fast as possible, with as few stoppages as possible, so they can accumulate as much surplus value as possible. Any interruption to the circuit stops the circulating elements acting as capital because capital is the circuit, the movement, the process itself rather than the elements entering and leaving it. If circulation stops, machines lie unused, workers become unemployed, commodities remain unsold and - what matters to the capitalist - no surplus value is produced.

The circulation of capital needs a **supply chain** of commodities. On the one hand, capitalists need to ensure this supply chain has enough commodities in it to ensure that production, circulation and consumption continue uninterrupted. On the other hand, capitalists want to reduce the supply chain to a minimum as the capital tied up as commodity capital waiting in supply chains produces no surplus value. If capital is stuck as one form of capital it stops circulating, leaving labour power and means of production that could be producing surplus value lying idle.

Capitalists need to buy new machines to replace obsolete machines and to expand production. The proportions between labour power and means of production are determined by the concrete labour needed for the labour process that produces particular commodities - if a capitalist wants to expand production they may have to wait until they have enough surplus value to buy an expensive new means of production, say a factory. Until then, the capitalist hoards this surplus value as a **reserve fund** of money capital which cannot act as capital until it buys means of production.

Capitalist accumulation spreads commodity production across the globe. The development of transport and communications reduces the cost of transporting commodities to market. The expansion of markets and sources of raw materials and machinery makes the supply of means of production more reliable, reducing the amount of commodities needed in the supply chain.

Commodities that are the output of feudalism, slavery and other non-capitalist modes of production enter into the circuit of industrial capital by being bought as means of production, means of subsistence or luxuries. Money from non-capitalist societies is used to buy commodities produced by capitalist production, bringing the products of non-capitalist societies into the circuit of industrial capital. **Commodification** and the rule of capital spreads across the world.

'With the development of capitalist production, the scale of production is determined less and less by the direct demand for the product and more and more by the amount of capital available in the hands of the individual capitalist, by the urge of self-expansion inherent in his capital and by the need of continuity and expansion of the process of production'.

Use values and value are only created in spheres of production. However a commodity is only useful once it is available for sale. Labour spent on the transport of commodities between their production and their point of sale is therefore productive labour carried out by productive workers that adds use value and value to commodities.

The labour of **commercial workers** is spent buying, advertising, marketing and selling commodities rather than producing use values or value. As this labour adds no value to commodities it is unproductive labour. It is a necessary **circulation cost** for capital that only exists because commodities have to be exchanged for money before they can be consumed. The wages of commercial workers are a deduction from the surplus value produced by productive labour.

As with productive workers, unproductive workers labour part of their time for nothing. This surplus labour does not produce value but it does reduce the capitalist's circulation costs by the amount of surplus labour carried out so that 'a smaller part of society's labour-power and labour-time is tied up in this unproductive function'.

Although circulation costs are unproductive expenses from the standpoint of society, those capitalists who take on the role of selling the products of productive capital take a cut of the surplus value produced by productive workers. This is discussed further in *Part 15 Commerce*.

Working class struggles in the 20th century forced some richer capitalist countries to provide workers with free health services, free higher education, pensions, unemployment benefits and welfare. This increased the number of unproductive workers providing services to meet social needs rather than produce surplus value.

These gains have been whittled away ever since, with welfare for the poorest, whose existence means nothing to capital, increasingly left to charity and neglect. For capitalists, the privatisation and commodification of education, health and other state services turns unproductive public service workers into productive exploited workers, employed to expand capital rather than to meet social needs.

In a socialist society there would be no distinction between productive and unproductive labour as all labour would be about meeting social needs rather than producing and reproducing capital. Health, education and caring services would expand while the unproductive labour of commercial workers would disappear.

10 Turnover time

The performance of a circuit of industrial capital is called a **turnover** of capital. The length of time this circuit takes is the **turnover time** of that capital.

The part of the turnover time capital spends in a sphere of production is called **production time**. The production time of a commodity is made up of **labour time** when the labour process is being carried out and value is being produced and **waiting time** when production is interrupted or the commodity has to be left to undergo natural processes of growth or change. This waiting time is often determined by natural laws and can be shortened by the application of technology.

The part of the turnover time capital spends in the sphere of circulation is called **circulation time**. This is made up of **buying time** when means of production have been bought and are waiting to be used in production and **selling time** when produced commodities are waiting to be sold. Commodities that are services provided at the same time as they are bought do not have a selling time.

The only part of the turnover time that capitalists want to lengthen is surplus labour time, that part of labour time when workers produce surplus value. Capitalists want to reduce not just the worker's necessary labour time but also any waiting time, buying time or selling time as no value or surplus value is produced during these times.

Productive capital that transfers all its value to a commodity in one turnover is called **circulating capital**. Labour power, raw materials and auxiliary goods are circulating capital. Productive capital that transfers its value to commodities over more than one turnover is called **fixed capital**. Tools, machines and buildings are fixed capital. As fixed capital only transfers some of its value each turnover, it has a longer turnover time than circulating capital.

The faster a capital can perform a turnover of circulating capital and start another one, the more surplus value it produces. The turnover time of any capital affects how much surplus value it can produce in a period of time independently of the rate of exploitation.

As capital accumulates and expands into new markets, the average distance between where commodities are produced and where they are consumed grows, increasing turnover times. At the same time as accumulation leads to longer turnover times, capitalists reduce turnover times as far as possible by improving transport and communications with new routes and faster forms of transport, cutting the length of time commodities take to get to their destination.

The money capital needed to continue production on the same scale as before, the capitalist's **tied up capital**, grows as turnover times lengthen and more capital is tied up during longer selling and buying times. A reduction in turnover time releases some of this capital.

Released capital is capital that had to be used as productive capital up to a certain time but has become superfluous for production to continue on the same scale because of increased productivity. As productivity increases, the amount of released capital in circulation expands. Alongside real accumulation, hoards of **reserve money capital** are accumulated or, as we will see in *Part 16 Interest and fictitious capital*, lent to other capitalists at a price.

Some surplus value must always exist as money so a portion of society's labour power and means of production are spent producing the money material, gold. As gold is already money, **gold capitalists** do not need to realise the surplus value produced by workers in the gold industry (C'-M') making the **circuit of gold production** M-C (L + MP) ... P ... M'. While industrial capitalists take more money out of circulation than they put in, gold capitalists put more money into circulation than they take out.

When workers win wage rises, the total amount of money in circulation is not affected by this redivision of the value of the product between workers and capitalists. A rise in wages 'does not promote an increase in the prices of the necessities of life but simply displaces buyers of luxuries. More luxuries than before are consumed by labourers, and relatively fewer by capitalists'. 'If it were in the power of the capitalist producers to raise the prices of their commodities at will, they could and would do so without a rise in wages... The capitalist class would never resist the trades' unions, if it could always... avail itself of every rise in wages in order to raise prices of commodities much higher yet.'

11 Reproduction

So far we have looked at how individual industrial capitalists produce and circulate commodities in their endless quest for surplus value. We have assumed that capitalists are able to buy the labour power and means of production they need and sell the commodities they produce at their direct prices. But how does this happen? How does capital as a whole reproduce itself?

Just as every individual capitalist is also a member of the capitalist class, every **individual capital** is 'a fraction endowed with individual life' of capital as a whole, the movement of the circuits of all individual capitals, all production, consumption and exchange. 'The circuits of the individual capitals intertwine, presuppose and necessitate one another, and form, precisely in this interlacing, the movement of the **total social capital**'.

To understand how capital as a whole reproduces itself at its most basic level, we look at one turnover of total social capital that takes one year in an economy with only productive workers and capitalists. We assume no change in productivity or the organic composition of capital during the year, that all constant capital is circulating capital used up in production during the year and that commodities exchange at their direct prices without credit or foreign trade.

The value of all the commodities produced by total social capital in a year, like the value of any commodity, consists of constant capital, variable capital and surplus value, $c + v + s$. This **total annual product** can be divided into two departments of social production making commodities with fundamentally different use values. **Department 1** makes means of production to be consumed in production. **Department 2** makes **consumer goods** to be consumed privately by workers and capitalists as means of subsistence or luxuries. The value of the total annual product can now be written as $1c + 1v + 1s + 2c + 2v + 2s$.

If we assume simple reproduction, where all surplus value is consumed privately by capitalists and there is no accumulation, how would these departments have to interact for total social capital to reproduce? The value of all means of production produced during the year ($1c + 1v + 1s$) would need to have the same value as all means of production consumed during the year ($1c + 2c$) and the value of all consumer goods produced during the year ($2c + 2v + 2s$) would need to have the same value as all consumer goods consumed by workers and capitalists during the year ($1v + 1s + 2v + 2s$).

For this to happen, department 1 capitalists would need to sell means of production to department 2 capitalists of the same value it takes to pay their workers' wages ($1v$) and their own surplus value ($1s$). Put another way, department 2 capitalists would need to sell consumer goods of the same value it takes to buy the constant capital ($2c$) they need.

In simple reproduction this **great exchange** can be written as $1v + 1s = 2c$. The capitalists of department 1 replace their own constant capital ($1c$) either by producing it themselves or buying it from other department 1 capitalists. Department 1's variable capital and surplus value ($1v + 1s$) buys consumer goods for department 1's workers and capitalists from department 2 capitalists who can then buy the constant capital ($2c$) they need. This process lies at the heart of capitalist economies.

In reality, because capital is self-expanding value that has to accumulate, capitalists do not privately consume all the surplus value their workers produce - they use some of it to buy constant and variable capital to expand production. Simple reproduction takes place as part of the expanded reproduction, or accumulation, of industrial capital.

For capital to accumulate, assuming no change in productivity, department 1 has to produce means of production with a greater value than $1c + 2c$, the value of means of production needed for simple production. As production in department 1 expands, the demand for consumer goods from department 1 workers and capitalists also expands, expanding production in department 2 to meet this demand.

Capital does not accumulate in a harmonious way. The reproduction of total social capital is a process 'so complicated that it offers ever so many occasions for running abnormally'. There are 'so many possibilities of crises, since a balance is itself an accident owing to the spontaneous nature of this production'.

Capitalist reproduction takes place on a world scale and is prone to disruption at every stage. A shortage of raw materials like oil or auxiliary goods like microchips can stop production in its tracks. Capitalists must also be able to find the labour power they need to produce anything. Shortages in other industries, the depletion of nature or natural disasters, climate change, pandemics, wars or even a ship stuck in the Suez Canal cause major disruption to capitalist accumulation that can lead to shortages of vital consumer goods such as food. Conscious disruption of capitalist reproduction in the form of strikes, factory occupations, blockades or other action that disrupts the circulation of capital hurt capitalists and can force them to concede workers' demands or go out of business.

Through constant **disproportionality** between departments of social production and branches of industry, commodities tend towards being produced in the proportions needed. If a branch of industry produces more commodities than are needed, the price of those commodities falls. If a branch of industry is not producing enough commodities to satisfy demand, the price of those commodities rises. Capital constantly flows from the overproducing branch of industry to the underproducing ones in search of as much surplus value as possible.

Underconsumptionism is the view that capitalism's regular crises are caused by one specific disproportion within the economy, workers not being able to buy enough commodities. This view is common amongst people who want to improve workers' living standards without abolishing capital. But exploitation of workers is the basis of capital. Workers will always get less than they produce while capital exists. 'Capitalist production comprises conditions independent of good or bad will, conditions which permit the working class to enjoy that relative prosperity only momentarily, and at that always only as the harbinger of a coming crisis'.

While capitalist crises always take the form of

capitalists being unable to sell the commodities they produce, 'it is sheer tautology to say that crises are caused by the scarcity of effective consumption, or of effective consumers'. 'If one were to attempt to give this tautology the semblance of a profounder justification by saying that the working class receives too small a portion of its own product and the evil would be remedied as soon as it receives a larger share of it and its wages increase in consequence, one could only remark that crises are always prepared by precisely a period in which wages rise generally and the working class actually gets a larger share of that part of the annual product which is intended for consumption'. It is not a lack of consumption by workers that forces capitalism into periodic crises. We will find out in *Part 14 The falling rate of profit* what does.

12 Profit

Part 12 starts the third volume of *Capital* which looks at how the laws governing value, surplus value and capital established in the first and second volume express themselves in everyday life.

'The various forms of capital, as evolved in this book, thus approach step by step the form which they assume on the surface of society, in the action of different capitals upon one another, in competition, and in the ordinary consciousness of the agents of production themselves'.

In particular, the third volume looks at how society's total surplus value is divided up between different kinds of capitalists and landowners.

We have seen that the value of any commodity is made up of the value of the dead labour transferred to the commodity during its production (constant capital) and the value added by living labour during production (variable capital and surplus value), c + v + s.

But capitalists do not know or care about value or surplus value. They are only interested in turning money into more money, M-C-M'. As far as capitalists are concerned, the money it costs them to pay wages and buy the means of production to make a commodity (c + v) is the commodity's **cost price**, the price they sell a commodity at (c + v + s) is the commodity's selling or **market price** and the difference, the surplus value (s), is their **profit**.

Capitalists do care about the cost price they pay to produce commodities and, most of all, they care about the profit they make. If capitalists sell the commodities their workers produce below their cost price they will soon go out of business because they will not make a profit. If they sell commodities above their cost price they will make a profit whether the selling price is above or below the commodity's direct price that reflects its value, a price they are unaware of.

This means that the profit an individual capitalist makes can be more or less than the surplus value produced by their workers. We will see the importance of this in parts 13 to 17 where we look at how the surplus value initially produced by workers for industrial capitalists is shared with other capitalists and landowners.

As profit is the excess of a commodity's selling price over its cost price, it appears to arise from investing in constant capital as much as from investing in variable capital to buy the living labour that is the sole source of profit. 'While surplus value and profit are actually the same thing and numerically equal, profit is nevertheless a converted form of surplus value, a form in which its origin and the secret of its existence are obscured and extinguished'.

Since 'in reality, under competition, in the actual market, it depends on market conditions whether or not and to what extent this surplus is realised', the 'illusion' is created that 'the surplus value incorporated in a commodity is not realised through its sale, but springs out of the sale itself'.

Profit appears to result from the productive power of capital itself and the actions of the capitalists who represent capital, rather than from surplus labour. It appears 'that capital generates this new value by its movement in the processes of production and circulation. But the way in which this occurs is cloaked in mystery and appears to originate from hidden qualities inherent in capital itself'.

Capitalists want to make the highest **rate of profit** possible from the capital they invest in production. The rate of profit is the ratio between the surplus value (s) produced by workers and the **total capital** (C) a capitalist invests in production to create this surplus value, s / c + v or s / C. The rate of profit measures the rate at which capital expands. The pursuit of the highest possible rate of profit is what drives capital and capitalists.

A capital's rate of profit is partly determined by its rate of exploitation (s / v). If the rate of exploitation rises, the rate of profit rises too. However, as the rate of profit is measured against constant and variable capital rather than just variable capital, the higher the value of the constant capital the lower the rate of profit (s / c + v). As there is always some constant capital used in production, the rate of profit is always lower than the rate of exploitation.

The **annual rate of profit** is the ratio of profit produced in a year to the total capital employed in a year. This rate is calculated by multiplying the rate of profit by the number of turnovers that variable capital, the capital that produces surplus value and profit, makes in a year. If there is one turnover of variable capital per year, the rate of profit and the annual rate of profit will be the same. If there are more or less than one turnover a year the annual rate of profit will be higher or lower than the rate of profit.

While increasing the rate of exploitation depends on reducing the cost of variable capital, wages, increasing the rate of profit also depends on reducing the cost of constant capital by making **economies** in its use. Reducing the cost of production by running machinery at dangerous speeds at the expense of workers' safety, making workplaces more crowded and making changes or introducing machines that make the labour process more efficient all reduce the cost of constant capital, and therefore increase the rate of profit, without affecting the rate of exploitation.

The price of raw materials becomes more important as productivity increases and the value of the labour power and fixed capital needed to produce each commodity falls. The rate of profit rises when the cost of raw materials falls and falls when the cost of raw materials rises.

When raw materials or energy become expensive, capitalists try to regulate their production to ensure accumulation can continue. However as soon as raw materials become affordable again 'all thought of a common, all-embracing and far-sighted control of the production of raw materials gives way once more to the faith that demand and supply will mutually regulate one another. And it must be admitted that such control is on the whole irreconcilable with the laws of capitalist production, and remains for ever a pious wish, or is limited to exceptional co-operation in times of great stress and confusion'.

We saw in *Part 2 Capital and labour power* that capital develops 'a life-process of its own' as it turns capitalists' money into more money by exploiting labour in the labour process. While production to meet the needs of producers has limits, 'the circulation of money as capital is, on the contrary, an end in itself, for the expansion of value takes place only within this constantly renewed movement. The circulation of capital has therefore no limits'.

Capital's need to constantly expand itself by absorbing surplus value is reflected in capitalists' need to increase their profits without limits. The pursuit of profit by capitalists is an end in itself, driving increases in productivity, increased exploitation of labour and the destruction of nature.

Climate change increases the costs of labour power, energy and raw materials and is therefore a threat to capitalists' profits. Capitalists will try to reduce these costs by cutting wages, demanding cheap fossil fuels and devastating nature. The rest of us will have to decide whether we accept a future based on capital's priorities or whether we overthrow capital and establish a classless society based on meeting human needs.

13 Competition

As we have considered things up till now, each individual industrial capital has its own rate of exploitation, organic composition and average turnover time and so its own rate of profit. We have mainly assumed that each commodity has the value it takes to produce it and sells at its direct price.

We saw in *Part 12 Profit* that the profit an individual capitalist makes can be more or less than the surplus value produced by their workers. If a capitalist sells commodities above their cost price they will make a profit whether the selling price is above or below the commodity's direct price that reflects its value, a price they are unaware of.

Capitals with higher organic compositions of capital and therefore higher productivity can produce commodities with less labour and therefore a lower value and lower direct price. When a capitalist does this they make a **surplus profit**, a profit above the average.

Capitalists with lower productivity need more labour to produce each commodity so have to sell their commodities below their direct prices. They still make a profit but less than they would if their commodities sold at their direct price.

To the extent that capital is mobile, **competition** between capitals with different organic compositions of capital leads to a continual transfer of capital from capitals with lower compositions to capitals with higher ones in search of surplus profit.

The cost prices capitalists pay to produce commodities depends entirely on the outlay of capital that is needed within their branch of industry. However the transfer of capital from less profitable to more profitable branches of industry as capitalists seek out more profit tends to level all rates of profit through **profit equalisation** of capitals with different organic compositions.

This equalisation creates an **average rate of profit** where each individual capital makes a profit in proportion to its size. Each individual capitalist's workers produces surplus value not directly for the capitalist exploiting them but for all capitalists.

This constant flow of capital from branches of industry with lower rates of profit to branches of industry with higher rates of profit tends to transform direct prices into **production prices** or prices of production, the price commodities sell at if the capital producing them earns the average rate of profit.

Production prices diverge from direct prices. The production price of a commodity made by a more productive labour process will be above its direct price while the production prices of a less productive labour process will be below its direct price.

Market prices tend to fluctuate around production prices rather than direct prices. If demand for a commodity is satisfied by the supply of commodities at their production price, the market price will be the same as its production price. If the supply of a commodity is less than the demand for it, the market price will rise above the production price and more capitalists will start to produce the commodity, driving the market price down again. If the supply of a commodity is more than the demand for it, its market price will drop below its production price and some capitalists will stop producing the commodity, driving the market price up again.

The transformation of direct prices into production prices takes place in the sphere of circulation, redistributing value between capitals in different branches of industry without affecting the total surplus value produced. The sum of the production prices of all commodities is the same as the sum of their direct prices but is redivided by competition. Production prices are therefore not determined by the value of any one commodity, but by the total value of all commodities.

The tendency towards an average rate is profit for all capitalists acts in a 'very complicated and approximate manner', as 'a never ascertainable average of ceaseless fluctuations'. The transfer of fixed capital used in one branch of production to another can be difficult or impossible so the equalisation of the rate of profit will be less evident in older investments where huge amounts of capital are tied up in the form of fixed capital.

The tendency towards an average rate of profit further obscures profit's source in living, surplus labour. The fact that investing in machines tends to raise profits rather than reduce them makes the source of profit appear as the opposite of what it is, so that 'the final pattern of economic relations as seen on the surface, in their real existence and consequently in the conceptions by which the bearers and agents of these relations seek to understand them, is very much different from, and indeed quite the reverse of, their inner but concealed essential pattern and the conception corresponding to it'.

Although production prices deviate from direct prices, they are still regulated by the law of value. 'Since the total value of the commodities regulates the total surplus-value, and this in turn regulates the level of average profit... it follows the law of value regulates the prices of production'.

Just as individual capitalists can make more or less profit than the surplus value produced by their workers, capitalists in richer countries with higher productivity can make profit at the expense of capitalists in poorer countries with lower productivity. This allows capitalists in more productive countries to take a share of the surplus value produced by workers in less productive countries through international trade.

This unequal exchange of labour between higher and lower productivity countries lies at the heart of **imperialism**, the division of the world into a few rich, high tech **imperialist countries** and lower tech, lower productivity **dominated countries** that are home to 85% of the world's population.[1] The transfer of wealth from dominated to imperialist countries has been estimated at over $10 trillion a year, a quarter of the production of imperialist countries.[2] This division of the world between a few mainly white imperialist countries and the rest of the world that started with colonialism and continues today using different means is the basis of **racism**.

We saw in *Part 4 Productivity* that colonialism created an international division of labour 'suited to the requirements of the chief centres of modern industry'. These requirements have seen the wealth ratio between rich and poor countries increase from around 4 to 1 before colonialism to more than 40 to 1 today.[3] The international division of labour has developed alongside colonialism, unequal exchange and the centralisation of capital described in *Part 7 Accumulation* to create huge transnational **corporations** mainly based in the imperialist countries that carry out 80% of world trade.[4]

These corporations dominate the **international labour process** by monopolising advanced technology and controlling the supply chains of most internationally traded production. They use investment, loans, licence fees, service payments, intellectual property rights, **transfer pricing**, where corporations buy parts below their full cost from foreign subsidiaries, and a host of other mechanisms to maximise their profitability. Over the last half century these corporations have moved the majority of the world's production of surplus value from imperialist countries to dominated ones where wages are lower and profits higher.[5]

14 The falling rate of profit

In *Part 2 Capital and labour power* we saw that capital is self-expanding value, that it is in capital's nature to grow. In *Part 7 Accumulation* we saw that as capital grows and accumulates, labour becomes more productive and the organic composition of capital rises. 'The same number of labourers, in the same time, i.e., with less labour, convert an ever-increasing quantity of raw and auxiliary materials into products, thanks to the growing application of machinery and fixed capital in general'.

What does this mean for capitalists' profits, 'the motive power of capitalist production'?

We saw in *Part 12 Profit* that the rate of profit is the ratio of surplus value (s) to the value of the capital invested to produce it (c + v). As labour becomes more productive, there is more dead labour (c) and less living labour (v + s), the only source of profit (s), in each commodity produced. 'The same process which brings about a cheapening of commodities in the course of the development of the capitalist mode of production, causes a change in the organic composition of the social capital invested in the production of commodities, and consequently lowers the rate of profit'.

Assuming a rate of exploitation (s / v) of 100% where half the value produced by workers is paid in wages and half taken as profit, we can see that as more of society's total social capital is invested in constant capital rather than variable capital, the average rate of profit falls.

20c + 80v + 80s = an average rate of profit of 80%
80c + 20v + 20s = an average rate of profit of 20%
95c + 5v + 5s = an average rate of profit of 5%

The **law of profitability** or the law of the tendency of the rate of profit to fall states that as productivity and the organic composition of capital rises, the rate of profit has a tendency to fall. The more capital grows, the lower the rate of that growth becomes. The fact that the rate of profit has a tendency to fall is '*an expression peculiar to the capitalist mode of production* of the progressive development of the social productivity of labour'. 'The rate of profit does not fall because labour becomes less productive, but because it becomes more productive'.

As capital accumulates and productivity increases, capitalists tend to make less profit from each commodity their workers produce but more profit overall by expanding the number of workers they employ. 'On the whole a relative decrease of variable capital and profit is accompanied by an absolute increase of both' so that 'the same laws produce for the social capital a growing absolute **mass of profit**, and a falling rate of profit'.

The increasing productivity that accompanies capitalist accumulation replaces living labour with dead labour in the labour process, reducing the rate of profit. However 'the same influences which produce a tendency in the general rate of profit to fall, also call forth counter-effects, which hamper, retard, and partly paralyse this fall. The latter do not do away with the law, but impair its effect'.

Anything that increases the rate of exploitation (s / v) increases the rate of profit (s / c + v). Capitalists who make the working day longer or intensify labour, for instance by speeding up production, increase the rate of exploitation and so the rate of profit. The rate of exploitation can also be increased by driving wages below the value of labour power, made possible by the reserve army of labour we read about in *Part 7 Accumulation*.

Increasing productivity not only reduces the rate of profit, it also reduces the value of commodities, including the commodities that make up the workers' means of subsistence. This allows capitalists to increase the rate of exploitation, and therefore the rate of profit, without reducing the amount of commodities workers can buy with their wages. However as the amount of living labour in commodities gets smaller, the effect a change in the rate of exploitation has on the rate of profit reduces.

The value of the elements of constant capital also falls as productivity increases and it becomes cheaper to produce them. This 'prevents the value of constant capital, although it continually increases, from increasing at the same rate as its material volume'.

The expansion of capital is accompanied by an even greater expansion of use values as the same amount of living labour is able to produce more use values by using cheaper raw materials and more productive machines. This depreciation of the elements of constant capital is 'another continually operating factor which checks the fall of the rate of profit' and plays an important role in crises.

As we saw in *Part 13 Competition*, capitalists in imperialist countries can increase their rate of profit through **foreign trade** with less productive countries, often ex-colonies, because of unequal exchange and a higher rate of exploitation in dominated countries. However the expansion of capitalist accumulation across the world increases the organic composition of capitals in the countries it exports capital to, making the rate of profit fall worldwide in the long run.

As capital accumulates, a portion of total social capital is invested in **infrastructure projects** necessary for economic expansion - railways are given as an example - that yield a low, steady rate of return to investors. These large, capital-intensive projects have particularly high organic compositions of capital and therefore particularly low rates of profit. These projects' profits are not included in the profit equalisation that determines the average rate of profit. If they were, the average rate of profit would be lower.

The exhaustion of natural resources reduces productivity. 'Productivity of labour is also bound up with natural conditions, which frequently become less productive as productivity grows'. 'Consider the mere influence of the seasons, for instance, on which the bulk of raw materials depends for its mass, the exhaustion of forest lands, coal and iron mines, etc'.

As productivity increases, living labour is replaced by machines in the labour process. The organic composition of capital rises, allowing more commodities to be produced, each with less value. This reduces the rate of profit while increasing the mass of profit. The **productive power of society** grows until the surplus value produced 'swells to immense dimensions'.

Surplus value does not become profit - what capitalists are after - until the commodity capital their workers produce has been sold at a profit and turned back into money capital. The ability of capitalists to do this is subject to the limits capitalist reproduction puts on the **consumer power of society**.

These limits 'reduce the consumption of the bulk of society to a minimum varying within more or less narrow limits' and is 'restricted by the tendency to accumulate, the drive to expand capital and produce surplus-value on an extended scale. This is law for capitalist production'.

Individual capitalists increase their production as far as their productive forces will allow, out of all proportion to the amount of money available to buy them. There is an **overproduction of capital** - too much commodity capital is produced to be sold at a profit - and the mass, as well as the rate, of profits falls.

Overproduction of capital does not mean that too many use values have been produced to meet human needs. 'There are not too many necessities of life produced, in proportion to the existing population. Quite the reverse. Too little is produced to decently and humanely satisfy the wants of the great mass'. Wealth that would meet human needs in a rational society causes the breakdown of reproduction in a capitalist one because commodities must be sold at a profit before they can be consumed.

'The *real barrier* of capitalist production is *capital itself*. Capital needs to increase its productivity, which reduces its value by depreciating current capital, and at the same time expand its value, because capital *is* expanding value. 'The means - unconditional development of the productive forces of society - comes continually into conflict with the limited purpose, the self-expansion of the existing capital'.

We saw in *Part 1 Commodities and money* that if producers cannot sell their commodities, the circulation of commodities and money is disturbed and a crisis can develop. This is what happens when capitalists can no longer sell the commodities their workers produce at a profit. 'The development of the productivity of labour creates out of the falling rate of profit a law which at a certain point comes into antagonistic conflict with this development and must be overcome constantly through crises'.

Huge quantities of produced commodity capital accumulate that cannot be sold at a profit but must be sold to pay debts. They are sold at a loss and market prices fall below cost prices. Accumulation stops, then goes into reverse. Some capital ceases to be capital as production is cut back. Variable capital is reduced as workers are laid off, increasing unemployment. Constant capital loses value and has to be depreciated or written off altogether as factories are closed and machines stop operating.

This depreciation of capital is not evenly spread between capitalists. Capitalists compete with each other to survive. Weaker capitalists go bankrupt and their assets are sold at a loss to surviving capitalists. Larger capitalists swallow smaller ones as their larger mass of profit allow them to survive off a lower rate of profit than smaller capitalists can. 'The class, as such, must inevitably lose. How much the individual capitalist must bear of the loss, *i.e.*, to what extent he must share in it at all, is decided by strength and cunning, and competition then becomes a fight among hostile brothers'.

The recession that follows a crisis sees depreciation, low levels of production and low prices create the conditions for a recovery. Capital is destroyed as elements of fixed capital are depreciated or abandoned. High unemployment forces workers to accept lower wages, increasing the rate of exploitation and rate of profit. Surviving capitalists buy up the assets of bankrupt capitals at rock bottom prices, centralising capital and concentrating production in more productive labour processes.

The depreciation of capital in the crisis and recession means that the same amount of surplus value now relates to a lower total capital. This reduces the organic composition of capital and raises the rate of profit again. Accumulation recovers as production for profit continues on a new, higher level, spiralling onto the next boom and the next crisis.

As capital becomes more concentrated it becomes 'an alienated, independent, social power, which stands opposed to society as an object, and as an object that is the capitalist's source of power'.

'The contradiction between the general social power into which capital develops, on the one hand, and the private power of the individual capitalists over these social conditions of production, on the other, becomes ever more irreconcilable, and yet contains the solution of the problem, because it implies at the same time the transformation of the conditions of production into general, common, social, conditions. This transformation stems from the development of the productive forces under capitalist production, and from the ways and means by which this development takes place.'

'Development of the productive forces of social labour is the historical task and justification of capital'. By increasing the productivity of human labour, capital 'unconsciously creates the material requirements of a higher mode of production' where humanity can meet its needs by organising production collectively.

Researchers have confirmed that capitalist accumulation leads to a rise in the organic composition of capital and a falling rate of profit. According to the *The Economist*, the average world rate of profit fell from 15% after World War Two to 10% in 1990 then 6% in 2017.[1] Across all the booms and crises between 1960 and 2019 the world organic composition of capital rose by about 0.8% a year, the world rate of exploitation rose by about 0.25% a year and the world rate of profit fell by about 0.5% a year.[2]

The law of the tendency of the rate of profit to fall as productivity increases 'testifies to the limitations and to the merely historical, transitory character of the capitalist mode of production; testifies that for the production of wealth, it is not an absolute mode, moreover, that at a certain stage it rather conflicts with its further development'.

15 Commerce

We have seen how in capitalist production surplus value appears as profit for individual industrial capitalists, how the rate of profit tends to equalise between individual capitalists and how the rate of profit tends to fall as the mass of profits grows. In the next three parts we look at how surplus value is divided up between different kinds of capitalists and landowners.

Industrial capitalists have to sell the commodities their workers produce if they are to make a profit. If they have to wait until the commodities they produce have been bought by their ultimate consumers, there would be an interruption in the reproduction of their capitals during circulation time while they wait to be paid, increasing their capital's turnover time and reducing their profit.

To avoid this, industrial capitalists reduce their turnover time by selling the commodities their workers produce to **commercial capitalists** at more than their cost price but less than their production price. Commercial capitalists centralise and economise the process of selling commodities so that instead of each industrial capitalist having to organise the sale of the commodities their workers produce to consumers these commodities are made available to consumers by commercial capitalists. The average rate of profit of industrial capital is reduced to allow commercial capital to make the average rate of profit too.

Commercial capital is capital functioning in the sphere of circulation. While the turnover of industrial capital involves the whole reproduction process of production and circulation, the turnover of commercial capital only involves buying commodities then selling them for more money than they were bought for. Commercial capital has the circuit M-C-M', buying commodities at one price then selling them at a higher one without any production taking place.

As we saw in *Part 9 Circulation*, the labour of commercial workers working for commercial capitalists reduces circulation costs but adds no value to commodities. Although commercial workers are unproductive of capital as a whole they are a source of profit to commercial capitalists who take a cut of the profits of industrial capitalists.

During the boom that precedes a crisis, industrial capitalists can keep selling the constantly expanding amount of commodities their workers produce to commercial capitalists for some time before it is discovered that they are not being sold to consumers and there has been an overproduction of commodities, production in excess of demand. The crisis occurs when commercial capitalists can no longer sell this growing amount of commodities at a profit and are forced to sell commodities at any price they can to get whatever money capital they can.

All capitalists need to keep a reserve fund of potential money capital to cope with disruptions to the expansion of their capital and to save for future investments. The cost of the safekeeping and movement of these reserve funds are costs of circulation necessary for industrial capitalists to function but not productive of surplus value. Just as commercial capitalists reduce the cost of circulation for industrial capitalists, **money dealing capitalists** reduce the cost of holding and moving money capital by centralising the storage and accounting of money.

By managing money for the capitalist class as a whole, money dealing capitalists make it easier for industrial and commercial capitalists - capitalists functioning in the reproduction of capital who together are called **functioning capitalists** and own **functioning capital** - to lend money to each other as **commercial credit** rather than hoard it. Once money dealing capitalists expand into lending their own money to functioning capitalists they become **money capitalists**, who we will investigate further in *Part 16 Interest and fictitious capital*.

Like the labour of buying and selling commodities, the labour of handling the exchange of money is unproductive labour that does not create surplus value. The money dealing capitalist's profit is a deduction from the surplus value taken from workers by industrial capitalists in the same way as the commercial capitalist's profit is deducted from the profits of industrial capitalists.

Commercial capital and money dealing capital have their origins in merchants' capital and usurers' capital, forms of capital we first came across in *Part 8 Origins*, that existed centuries before capitalist production became the dominant mode of production. Merchants of the first merchant towns and trading nations exploited the differences between the prices of products in non-capitalist societies and the higher prices they could sell these products at as commodities, appropriating a portion of the surplus product of non-capitalist communities mainly based on the production of use values. The activities of these merchants dissolved old relationships based on use value in these communities by increasing the circulation of money and subordinating production more and more to production of commodities for exchange.

The ratios in which products are exchanged for other products when they first become commodities is quite arbitrary. Continuity reduces this arbitrariness at first for the merchant, who compares prices and pockets the difference. As this trade develops, the law of value asserts itself.

The growth of world trade in the 16th and 17th centuries speeded up the transition from feudalism to capitalism. The products of colonised societies were turned into commodities supplying industrial capitalists in colonising countries with the raw materials they needed to expand and create new branches of industry. Once capitalist production became established on a large scale it created a market for itself by its ability to produce commodities with less labour. 'At this point commercial capital becomes the servant of industrial capital, for which continued expansion of the market becomes a vital necessity'.

16 Interest and fictitious capital

The money that functioning capitalists borrow from money capitalists to expand production is called **loan capital**. Money capitalists make a profit from loan capital by charging **interest** on the money they lend. As this interest must be repaid out of the functioning capitalist's profit, the **rate of interest** cannot be consistently higher than the functioning capitalist's rate of profit without them going out of business. Apart from this, interest rates are determined by the supply and demand for loan capital.

Loan capital seems to return more money than invested without any production taking place. 'It becomes a property of money to generate value and yield interest, much as it is an attribute of pear-trees to bear pears'. Loan capital becomes a commodity with the use value of producing profit by being invested in capitalist production.

The **circuit of loan capital** appears as M-M', money becoming more money. This circuit creates the fetishistic illusion that capital can expand itself without the need for workers to produce surplus value in the labour process.

But capital cannot create surplus value without

exploiting workers. The circuit M-M' is dependent on the functioning capitalist borrowing loan capital to produce new value in the circuit M-C … P … C'-M' and returning a portion of their M' to the money capitalist. Interest is part of the surplus value produced by workers' surplus labour and cannot exist unless surplus value is produced by workers. Money cannot create new value without production.

If the amount of money capital increases relative to productive capital, the interest rate falls and some money capitalists and rentiers become unable to live on their interest. They are forced to become functioning capitalists to make the same profit as before or, if all else fails, be forced to become workers. The profit that functioning capitalists are left with after paying interest on the loan capital they borrow is their **profit of enterprise**.

Functioning capitalists have to pay **wages of management** out of their profit of enterprise for the labour of managing and supervising production. As 'the work of supervision, divorced from the ownership of capital, is always readily obtainable' in return for wages of supervision it becomes 'useless for the capitalist to perform it himself'. The division between profits and salaries for the people running large companies becomes obscured as a hierarchy of control develops where 'boards of numerous managers or directors are placed above the actual director, for whom supervision and management serve only as a pretext to plunder the stockholders and amass wealth'.

Accumulation and centralisation of capital lead to the growth of **joint-stock companies** where individual capitalists swap control of their own capital for a share in larger capitals. Joint-stock companies separate management of production from the ownership of capital creating **social capital** as distinct from **private capital**, 'a new financial aristocracy, a new variety of parasites in the shape of promoters, speculators and simply nominal directors; a whole system of swindling and cheating by means of corporation promotion, stock issuance, and stock speculation. It is private production without the control of private property'.

'Instead of overcoming the antithesis between the character of wealth as social and as private wealth, the stock companies merely develop it in a new form' where 'control over social capital, not the individual capital of his own, gives him control of social labour'.

In **cooperative factories** where workers keep the profit made by their labour and managers are workers elected by other workers, the capitalist disappears as superfluous from the labour process. 'The co-operative factories of the labourers themselves represent within the old form the first sprouts of the new, although they naturally reproduce, and must reproduce, everywhere in their actual organisation all the shortcomings of the prevailing system. But the antithesis between capital and labour is overcome within them, if at first only by way of making the associated labourers into their own capitalist, i.e., by enabling them to use the means of production for the employment of their own labour. They show how a new mode of production naturally grows out of an old one, when the development of the material forces of production and of the corresponding forms of social production have reached a particular stage'.

As we saw in *Part 1 Commodities and money*, the circulation of money involves a circulation of credit between producers, where strings of debts cancel each other out without money changing hands. As capital accumulates, industrial capitalists move from selling commodities for money to exchanging them for **bills of exchange**, promises to pay money at a future date. This commercial credit reduces the cost of circulation by balancing out mutual claims, speeding up payments and in most cases eliminating the need for money as a means of payment.

Credit between functioning capitalists allows those with spare reserve money capital to lend it at interest to those who need it. This allows capital that would otherwise be hoarded as reserve funds to be directed to capitals in need of investment and used productively to create surplus value.

Capitalist reproduction depends on the existence of loan capital and credit. As long as capital accumulates, the credit system 'accelerates the material development of the productive forces and the establishment of the world-market'.

As capital accumulates, credit expands to meet the growing need for it. Commercial credit forms the basis of the **credit and banking system** where money capitalists and **bankers** become 'the general managers of money-capital', as both money dealing capitalists, processing payments for functioning capitalists, and money capitalists, taking in deposits and making loans.

Banks hold a reserve fund of money capital that is much smaller than the amounts of money they borrow or lend. As loans are only a transfer of money without a purchase, banks are able to lend out much more money than they borrow because they do not need to repay all the money deposited with them at any one time.

As credit expands, capital is created that has nothing to do with production. Loan capital invested in claims to future income that may or may not materialise is called **fictitious capital**. Fictitious capital is created by **capitalisation**, the transformation of potential future earnings into commodities with the use value of being able to give their owner a profit.

Fictitious capital takes many forms. Bonds, which we first came across in *Part 8 Origins*, are claims to a company's future profits or, in the case of bonds issued by states, claims against the state's future income. **Shares** are claims to the ownership and anticipated income of joint stock companies issued by these companies to raise capital. Shares are bought and sold on **stock markets** where their price is determined by speculation about the anticipated income of the capital invested in them. Every day billions of dollars, pounds and euros of fictitious capital are created and destroyed on various markets across the world.

Anything that capitalists can bet on can become fictitious capital. Bets on the prices of commodities, complex **financial instruments** and **cryptocurrencies** are all forms of fictitious capital that seem to make money out of nothing, with a price entirely determined by what investors believe it should be. Claims to future income from oil reserves that can never be extracted without inflicting enormous damage to our planet are fictitious capital that we must ensure become worthless.

To the extent that the accumulation of these claims expresses the accumulation of real capital it expresses the extension of the actual reproduction process. But as duplicates which are commodities, they are illusory, and 'their value may fall or rise quite independently of the movement of value of the real capital for which they are titles'. 'All connection with the actual expansion process of capital is thus completely lost, and the conception of capital as something with automatic self-expansion properties is thereby strengthened'.

In a boom, credit drives capitalist production 'beyond its own limits', allowing overproduction to continue much further than would be possible if commodities had to be paid for in cash. When the rate of profit of functioning capital falls, functioning capitalists **speculate** by investing in fictitious capital in search of surplus profit. Capitalists tend to invest in these speculative assets at the same stage of the industrial cycle, driving their prices up until they lose all connection with the profitability of capitalist production in a **speculative bubble**. This increase in the price of a commodity or group of commodities beyond any reason inevitably leads to the bubble bursting and prices collapsing - tulips in 1637,[1] financial assets of various kinds more recently - often triggering a crisis.

Credit maintains an illusory prosperity until the eve of the crisis. Once the overproduction hidden by selling on credit becomes obvious, industrial capitalists are forced to suddenly reduce production. Capitalists are not able to pay their debts and commercial credit breaks down. Owners of fictitious capital are forced to sell their shares and bonds for cash forcing their prices to fall, allowing larger capitals to buy them up cheap and increase the centralisation of capital.

The breakdown of credit in crises can make it appear that crises are caused by lack of credit rather than a crisis of capitalist production. 'The whole crisis seems to be merely a credit and money crisis' when 'in fact it is only a question of the convertibility of bills of exchange into money' in the circulation of industrial capital.

As we saw in *Part 1 Commodities and money*, money can be replaced in circulation by token money. The money we use in our everyday life is national currency, a form of token money. But token money only acts as a measure of value when it is backed by commodities of the same value it represents. If a country produces less, the **exchange rate** of its national currency with other currencies tends to fall because it represents less value.

Capital cannot put off crises by expanding credit forever. Wealth cannot be created by issuing banknotes or credit, only in the labour process. 'The entire artificial system of forced expansion of the reproduction process cannot, of course, be remedied by having some bank, like the Bank of England, give to all the swindlers the deficient capital by means of its paper and having it buy up all the depreciated commodities at their old nominal values'. Money, and therefore the money material, gold, will always be the foundation of the capitalist credit system. The credit system continually strives to overcome the **metal barrier** 'but again and again it breaks its back on this barrier'.

The claims of fictitious capital to future labour are now well beyond what can realistically be paid back. While world production has tripled in the last two decades, debt has multiplied five times.[2] At around \$300 trillion[3] world debt is more than three times annual world production.[4]

After the crisis of 2008, governments bailed out corporations with trillions of dollars of public money, turning money worth 50.4% of the world's annual production[5] from corporate debt into public debt. This transfer of debt to states saved large capitalists from bankruptcy and gave them trillions of dollars to speculate with at the cost of austerity for millions.

Poorer countries already have a debt crisis. Borrowing

costs for African countries are four times that in the United States[6] forcing the poorest countries in the world to spend more on interest payments than either education or health.[7] The external debt of low and middle-income economies has doubled in the last ten years while the debt of the poorest countries has nearly tripled forcing about 60% of the poorest countries into debt distress.[8]

When loan repayments become unpayable, companies, banks and countries default. It is impossible to predict what events in the world of fictitious capital will trigger future crises but it is certain that some will.

17 Rent

We have seen how the surplus value taken from workers by industrial capitalists is divided into profit for industrial and commercial capitalists and interest for money capitalists. However there is another major class in capitalist societies apart from the working class and the capitalist class, the class of landowners we last came across in *Part 8 Origins*, who claim a portion of surplus value by charging ground rent, what we will simply call **rent**.

Payment for the use of land in return for rent is older than capitalism. It exists whenever land is **landed property** owned by a class of landowners able to force those who work the land to pay them to do so, a premise common to all modes of production 'based on the exploitation of the masses in one form or another'.

Peasants producing goods on land belonging to feudal landowners had to produce a surplus over their own needs to pay rent to these landowners. They might do this by giving some of their produce to the landowner or working some of the time for the landowner on another piece of land. As peasants' products increasingly became commodities sold for money, rent increasingly becomes payable in money rather than in kind.

We saw in *Part 8 Origins* that the original accumulation of capital was based on the expulsion of the mass of rural producers from the land, their separation from the means to produce what they needed to survive. The peasants remaining on the land became wage workers labouring for capitalist farmers who in turn paid rent to landowners. Capitalist ground rent became the part of surplus value capitalists have to pay landowners to use their land for agriculture, mining, fishing, forestry or any other way of extracting use values from the land to make a profit.

In capitalist societies, landowners receive a part of surplus value simply by owning land. They play no part in the labour process that takes place on their land. Land simply means money to them, something that allows them to collect rent in return for allowing capitalist farmers to exploit workers on it. The connection between owning land and living and working on it is dissolved 'so thoroughly that the landowner may spend his whole life in Constantinople, while his estates lie in Scotland'.

The price of a piece of land is determined by capitalisation of the rent payable for that land in the same way that the price of shares and bonds are determined by their anticipated income. It is an imaginary price 'since the earth is not the product of labour and therefore has no value'.

Capitalists are unwilling to invest in land if their leases mean that any improvements they make become the property of the landowner when the lease ends. Agricultural production faces natural limits to increasing productivity that do not apply to industry. Organic and natural cycles such as the frequency of harvests or the life cycle of animals create barriers to the improvement of productivity that do not exist for the mechanical and chemical processes that industry depends on. These limitations mean that agriculture tends to have a lower organic composition of capital than industry, making the direct price of agricultural commodities higher than their production prices.

We saw in *Chapter 13 Competition* that profits tend to equalise as capital moves from less profitable branches of industry to more profitable ones. The existence of privately owned land prevents this equalisation by stopping the flow of capital into agriculture unless rent is paid to a landowner. Agricultural products are sold around their higher direct price rather than around a lower production price, with the landowner taking the difference in rent.

Labour employed by capital invested on land that is more fertile, has a better location or contains natural features such as accessible raw materials or waterfalls that produce cheap energy, is more productive than labour employed on less productive land. The same labour always produces the same value in the same amount of time, but the amount of use values labour produces in a given time depends on the labour's productivity.

This extra productivity allows capitalists investing on more productive land to make a surplus profit. The land does not add value because 'the earth is not the product of labour and therefore has no value'. All or some of this surplus profit is claimed by the landowner as **differential rent**.

'Landed property does not create the portion of value which is transformed into surplus-profit, but merely enables the landowner, the owner of the waterfall, to coax this surplus-profit out of the pocket of the manufacturer and into his own'.

Differential rent takes the form of **differential rent 1** based on the difference between the same amount of capital invested on different types of land and **differential rent 2** based on different amounts of capital invested in the same types of land.

Landowners will only rent land to a capitalist if they receive rent in return. Capitalists will only invest on poor land if they can make the average rate of profit. The owners of poor land that does not attract differential rent are able to charge **absolute rent** when the direct price of a crop grown on the land is higher than what its production price would have been if profit equalisation had applied. The crop is sold at its direct price, allowing the capitalist to make the average profit and the landowner to get rent.

Rent that originates from a market price being higher than either a direct price or production price is **monopoly rent** derived solely from a **monopoly price** of the produced commodities. This price is determined solely by the buyers' ability and willingness to pay it.

'The price of things which have in themselves no value, i.e., are not the product of labour, such as land, or which at least cannot be reproduced by labour, such as antiques and works of art by certain masters, etc., may be determined by many fortuitous combinations. In order to sell a thing, nothing more is required than its capacity to be monopolised and alienated'.

It is no surprise that capitalist agriculture has led to soil degradation, a collapse of biodiversity and our current ecological crises. 'The whole spirit of capitalist production, which is directed toward the immediate gain of money are in contradiction to agriculture, which has to minister to the entire range of permanent necessities of life required by the chain of successive generations'.

Production for profit means that exploitation and squandering of the vitality of the soil 'takes the place of conscious rational cultivation of the soil as eternal communal property, an inalienable condition for the existence and reproduction of a chain of successive generations of the human race'.

It is in the nature of capital to expand production beyond all natural and social limits. 'Large-scale industry and large-scale mechanised agriculture work together. If originally distinguished by the fact that the former lays waste and destroys principally labour-power, hence the natural force of human beings, whereas the latter more directly exhausts the natural vitality of the soil, they join hands in the further course of development in that the industrial system in the countryside also enervates the labourers, and industry and commerce on their part supply agriculture with the means for exhausting the soil'.

But there is nothing natural about the ownership of land by landowners. It only exists in capitalism because the capitalist class, many of whom are themselves landowners, allows landowners to get a cut of the value produced by workers on the basis that they 'own' land.

'From the standpoint of a higher economic form of society, private ownership of the globe by single individuals will appear quite as absurd as private ownership of one man by another. Even a whole society, a nation, or even all simultaneously existing societies taken together, are not the owners of the globe. They are only its possessors, its usufructuaries, and, like *boni patres familias*, they must hand it down to succeeding generations in an improved condition'.

18 Appearance and reality

We saw in *Part 3 Exploitation* how the value created by workers in capitalist production is initially divided between wages for workers and surplus value for the capitalists exploiting them. In parts 13 to 17 we saw how this surplus value is divided up between various capitalists and landowners as profit or rent.

This is not how things appear on the surface of capitalist society. Commodity fetishism mystifies social relationships, making capitalism appear as natural and unchangeable rather than a stage in the development of society. To capitalists and mainstream economists, labour must be wage labour for which workers get paid 'fair' wages, the means of production must be capital owned by capitalists entitled to a 'fair' profit and land must be privately owned land, entitling landowners to a 'fair' rent.

'From the common viewpoint these distribution relations appear as natural relations, as relations arising directly from the nature of all social production, from the laws of human production in general'. Labour, capital and land appear not just as the source of revenue for workers, capitalists and landowners but as **factors of production** that together produce commodities.

Mainstream economics calls this appearance the **trinity formula** and takes it as its starting point. The trinity formula assumes that human productive activity must be wage labour, the means of production must be capital and land must be landed property. Any alternative is inconceivable, any deeper analysis pointless. Value and surplus value do not exist.

In reality, wages, profit and rent constitute the sources of income of the three main classes in capitalist society, workers, capitalists and landowners. Workers create wealth, capitalists exploit workers to take some of that wealth for themselves then give a cut to landowners.

But this is not a static situation. Capital's development of the productive forces, including the working class, leads to 'the creation of the elements for a new and higher form' of society where society as a whole plans and develops production to meet human needs 'with the least expenditure of energy and under conditions most favourable to, and worthy of, their human nature'.

Beyond the realm of **necessity** where people have to labour to reproduce themselves lies 'that development of human energy which is an end in itself, the true realm of **freedom**' which 'can blossom forth only with this realm of necessity as its basis.' Whether or not humanity reaches this realm of freedom depends on the success of the struggles of the vast majority of humanity against the capitalists and their allies who are preventing us from reaching it.

Want to discuss *Capital?*

Thanks for taking the time to read this book. I hope you found it worthwhile.

If you're interested in joining or helping to run an online or local reading group to discuss *Capital* with the help of *Capital Condensed* please get in touch at capitalcondensed.net. You will be contacted when groups are getting set up and sent details of other events that might be of interest. You can also get in touch with me through the website.

The more reviews a book gets on Amazon the wider audience it gets. Reviews also help readers decide whether a book is worth buying or not - and I'm always interested to read them. You can leave a review and read other readers' reviews of *Capital Condensed* on its Amazon reviews page.

Colin Chalmers

Categories

absolute limit see natural limit

absolute rent *absolute ground rent* rent paid to allow the use of land for production 17

absolute surplus value surplus value arising from lengthening or intensifying the working day 4

abstract labour *abstract human labour, homogeneous labour, general labour,* human labour as such 1

abstraction the development of categories by leaving out other aspects of reality in order to understand reality, introduction

accumulated labour see dead labour

accumulation fund see reserve fund

accumulation of capital *accumulation, concentration of capital, capitalist accumulation, extended reproduction, reproduction on an extended scale* the reproduction of capital where capitalists turn surplus value into capital 7

agricultural worker workers labouring in agriculture 8

alienation *estrangement* separation from 2

annual product see total annual product

annual rate of profit the ratio of profit produced in a year to the total capital employed in a year 12

anthropocene *capitalocene* our current geological age, one where human activity has a significant impact on our planetary ecological systems 4

associated producers people producing things of use and sharing them with each other, introduction

auxiliary good see intermediate good

average labour *homogenous labour, simple labour* labour of average ability and intensity 1

average rate of profit *general rate of profit, normal rate of profit* the rate of profit every capital receives when commodities are sold at their production price 13

average social labour the average labour performed by workers as part collective labour 4

bank an institution that borrows and lends money 8

banker an owner or senior manager of a bank 16

banknote a note issued by a bank promising to pay an amount of money when returned 1

bill of exchange credit between functioning capitalists 16

bond an agreement where a debtor borrows money from a creditor in return for interest payments and the repayment of the amount borrowed at a future date 8

boom *period of overproduction of capital* the period in the industrial cycle between recovery and a crisis when production reaches its highest point 7

bourgeois equality see formal equality

bourgeoisie see capitalist class

branch of industry *branch of production, sector of production, industrial sector* a part of industry producing particular types of commodities as part of the division of labour in society 4

business cycle see industrial cycle

buying time the time when capital exists as means of production not yet used in the labour process 10 capital advanced see original capital

capital self-expanding value 2

capitalisation the calculation of the price of a commodity from the amount of income that commodity is expected to earn 16

capitalism *capitalist mode of production* the private ownership and control of the means of production and distribution by the capitalist class based on the exploitation of the wage labour of the working class, introduction

capitalist accumulation see accumulation of capital

capitalist class *bourgeoisie* the class in capitalist society that owns the means of production and exists by exploiting the working class 3

capitalist crisis see crisis

capitalist farmer a capitalist who makes surplus value from the labour of agricultural workers 8

capitalist ground rent see rent

capitalist mode of production see capitalism

capitalist private property the means of production owned by capitalists 8

capitalist production *valorisation* the production of commodities with the purpose of producing surplus value for a capitalist 2

capitalist relationship *wage slavery* workers selling their labour power to capitalists in return for wages 7

capitalist reproduction see reproduction of capital

capitalist society a society where the capitalist mode of production is dominant 1

capitalist someone who owns means of production and exists by exploiting the working class 2

capitalocene see anthropocene

casualisation the change from workers having a definite

working week to being hired by the hour 6

category an aspect of reality abstracted in thought in order to understand the relations between different categories, introduction

centralisation of capital *consolidation of capital* The incorporation of smaller capitals into fewer large capitals 7

circuit of gold production the circuit of capital when the commodity produced is the money material and therefore has no need to be realised 10

circuit of industrial capital *circuit of productive capital* the circuit of capital involving capitalist production 9

circuit of loan capital the circuit of capital that a money capitalist lends to an industrial capitalist in return with for interest 16

circulating capital *fluid capital* capital invested in labour power and means of production that is incorporated in each commodity as it is produced 10

circulation cost a cost a capitalist pays to sell their commodities 9

circulation of capital the movement of capital between its different forms 2

circulation of commodities the circulation of commodities as they are bought and sold 1

circulation of credit the circulation of debts 1

circulation of matter *metabolism* interactions within nature that allow the reproduction of life 4

circulation of money *currency of money* the circulation of money as it is used to buy and sell commodities 1

circulation time *time of circulation* the part of the circuit of industrial capital when commodities are in the sphere of circulation 10

class a group of people who share a similar relationship to the means of production, introduction

class struggle the struggle between classes 3

classical economics *classical political economy* the scientific study of capitalist society based on the law of value from the late 17th century to the middle of the 19th century 1

classical political economy see classical economics

collective labour the labour of a group of workers labouring together to produce the same sort of commodity 4

collective machine machines operating together in the labour process 4

collective production *socialised production* production by associated producers 8

collective property *socialised property* common ownership of the means of the production 8

collective worker *collective labourer* a group of workers labouring together to produce the same sort of commodity 4

collective working day *combined working day* the combined working day of a large group of workers labouring together to produce the same sort of commodity 4

colonialism *the colonial system* direct control of a people, land or country by a foreign country 4

combined working day see collective working day

commercial capital *trading capital* capital functioning in the sphere of circulation by buying and selling commodities 15

commercial capitalist *merchant capitalist, trading capitalist* a capitalist who buys commodities to sell at a profit 15

commercial credit credit between functioning capitalists 15

commercial war *trade war* war between countries caused

by conflicting economic interests 8

commercial worker an unproductive worker in the sphere of circulation 9

commodification the transformation of life into the production and exchange of commodities 9

commodity a product of human labour produced for exchange 1

commodity capital capital in the form of non-money commodities 9

commodity fetishism the appearance that commodities have power over people 1

commodity production the production of commodities by human labour 1

commodity supply see supply chain

communism see socialism

competition the process that forces individual capitalists to conform to capital's need to expand 13

composition of capital see organic composition of capital

concentration of capitalism see accumulation of capital

concrete labour *useful labour, specific labour* a specific type of human labour that produces a specific use value 1

constant capital capital invested in means of production that do not change their value during the labour process 3

consumer good *means of consumption, articles of consumption* a commodity produced for individual consumption 11

consumer power of society what a society produces 14

contradiction conflict between opposites, the means by which reality changes and develops, introduction

cooperation a large group of workers labouring together to produce the same sort of commodity under the control of a capitalist 4

cooperative factory a factory owned and run by workers 16

corporation large company 13

cost price *capitalist cost, target cost* the cost to capitalists of the labour power and means of production they buy to produce new commodities 12

credit and banking system banks and capital markets 16

credit money owed to a creditor by a debtor, same as debt 1

creditor someone who is owed money 1

crisis breakdown in the circulation of commodities and money; after *Part 1 Commodities and Money* also a capitalist crisis, the form taken by this breakdown in circulation involving capitalist production as the period in the industrial cycle between boom and recession 1

cryptocurrency digital currency based on cryptographic security that is independent of states 16

crystallised labour see dead labour

currency of money see circulation of money

dead labour *past labour, embodied labour, objectified labour, accumulated labour, crystallised labour, materialised labour* living labour that has been objectified as value in commodities 3

debt money owed by a debtor to a creditor, same as credit 1

debtor someone who owes money 1

department 1 branches of industry making means of production 11

department 2 branches of industry making consumer goods 11

depreciation see physical depreciation and moral depreciation

depression see recession

destitute surplus population *pauperism* workers suffering destitution 7

differential rent rent paid for the use of more productive land

differential rent 1 differential rent paid for the use of more fertile land 17

differential rent 2 differential rent paid for the use of land that is more productive because of capital invested on it 17

direct price the price of a commodity when money material with the same value has the same price 1

disproportionality production in different departments or branches of industry being out of proportion 11

division of labour by region *territorial division of production* the division of labour between different geographical regions 4

division of labour in production *technical division of labour* the division of the labour process into different tasks performed by different workers 4

division of labour in society *social division of labour* the division of a society's total labour into different types of labour producing different use values 1

domestic industry *petty industry* production carried out in homes 8

domestic labour *domestic work, reproductive labour* unpaid labour carried out privately to reproduce labour power (domestic labour is also used in *Capital* to refer to wage labour carried out at home rather than in a factory) 2

domestic work see domestic labour

dominated countries all countries except imperialist ones 13

economies savings in the use of constant capital in the labour process 12

embodied labour see dead labour

enclosure the transformation of common land into the privately owned land of a few landowners 8

energy source *prime mover* the source of energy for the labour process 4

equivalent form of value the form of value a commodity has when its use value expresses the value of another commodity 1

excess production time see waiting time

exchange rate *rate of exchange* the ratios of exchange between national currencies 16

exchange swap 1

exchange value *form of value, value form* the form that value takes in societies based on commodity production and exchange 1

expropriation the theft of land from producers living off the land 8

extended reproduction see accumulation of capital

factors of production land, labour and capital, the three things needed to produce commodities according to mainstream economics 18

factory a place where workers and machines produce commodities 4

feudalism *the feudal system* a mode of production based on small producers working land in exchange for providing labour or products to a landowner 8

fiat money token money in the form of a national currency 1

fictitious capital *imaginary money wealth* capital invested in claims to future surplus value that may or may not materialise 16

financial capitalist see money capitalist

financial instrument a contract that creates a financial asset and a financial liability such as a bond or share 16

financier see money capitalist

fixed capital constant capital that transfers its value as a means of production to commodities over time through wear and tear 10

floating surplus population workers who move in and out of work and who are currently unemployed 7

fluid capital see circulating capital

forces of production the objects, systems, technologies, skills and labour that produce use values 8

foreign trade trade between countries 14

form of value see exchange value

formal equality *bourgeois equality* the exchange of commodities, including labour power, for other commodities of the same value; the illusion of equality between people that this exchange gives 7

formal subsumption the production of commodities by workers for capitalists in return for wages 5

free time time when someone is not labouring or reproducing their labour power 5

freedom the development of human energy as an end in itself on the basis of associated producers rationally regulating their relationships with the rest of nature 18

functional depreciation see moral depreciation

functioning capital *real capital* industrial or commercial capital 15

functioning capitalist industrial or commercial capitalist 15

general formula for capital in circulation money becoming commodities becoming more money 2

general law of capitalist accumulation see law of capitalist accumulation

general rate of profit see average rate of profit

gold capitalist a capitalist employing workers to mine gold 10

gold the element that is the most widely used money material 1

great exchange the sale of means of production by capitalists producing them to capitalists producing consumer goods 11 ground rent see rent

guild association of merchants or skilled workers 8

hoard money withdrawn from circulation 1

human labour power see labour power

imaginary price *irrational price* a price given to something with no value 1

imperialism the domination of the world by a few imperialist countries 13

imperialist countries countries with high technology companies that consistently appropriate value from dominated countries 13

individual capital a fraction of total social capital 11

individual consumption the consumption of commodities by individuals 7

individual private property means of production owned by individuals and families 8

individual production production carried out by individuals and families 8

individual value the value a commodity would have if it was based on the labour time an individual producer needs to produce it 4

industrial capital *productive capital* capital invested in capitalist production to produce surplus value 9

industrial capitalist *productive capitalist* a capitalist employing workers to produce surplus value 9

industrial cycle *business cycle, trade cycle* the cyclical appearance of periods of boom, crisis, recession and recovery as capital develops 7

industrial sector see branch of industry

industry *modern industry* production of commodities using cooperation, the division of labour and machines 4

infrastructure project a project contributing to the basic structure of the economy 14

instrument of labour a tool, thing or process used to transform the objects of labour into new use values during the labour process 3

intellectual labour *mental labour* labour carried out by thinking rather than physical motion 4

intensity of labour how hard a worker labours 1

interest bearing capital see loan capital

interest rate see rate of interest

interest regular payments at a predetermined rate from a borrower to a lender of an amount above the amount borrowed in return for a loan 16

intermediate good *auxiliary good, partly-finished good, producer good, component* a commodity produced by labour out of raw materials for use as an object of labour in the labour process 3

intermediate subsumption the production of commodities for capitalists by independent producers outside the circuit of capital 5

international division of labour the worldwide division of labour between different countries 4

international labour process the labour process that produces commodities to be sold across the world 13

international value the value of a commodity on the world market 6

irrational price see imaginary price

joint-stock company a company that is owned by its shareholders 16

labour *human labour* purposeful human activity aimed at producing something of use 1

labour power *human labour power, labour capacity* a human being's vitality and creative abilities 2

labour process *production process, direct process of production* the process where human beings interact with other elements of nature to produce use values 3

labour time *working period, working time* the time when labour and means of production produce commodities 10

labourer see worker

landed property property owned by a landowner 17

landowner an owner of land 8

latent surplus population workers not yet integrated into capitalist production 7

law of capitalist accumulation *law of accumulation, general law of capitalist accumulation* the law that as capital accumulates and centralises, the organic composition of capital rises and the amount of living labour needed to produce commodities falls 7

law of profitability *law of the tendency of the rate of profit to fall* the law that as productivity increases in a capitalist society, the profit made from each produced commodity tends to fall 14

law of the tendency of the rate of profit to fall see law of profitability

law of value *law of the value of commodities* the law that the value of a commodity is determined by the amount of socially necessary labour time needed to reproduce it 1

legislation laws passed by states 3

living labour workers' labour that adds value to commodities during the labour process 3

loan capital *loanable capital, loanable money capital, interest bearing capital, moneyed capital, borrowed capital* money lent by money capitalists to industrial and commercial capitalists to be used as capital 16

luxury *luxury goods* a commodity consumed by capitalists on top of their means of subsistence 4

machine an instrument of labour that performs simple or complex tasks in the labour process using a single energy source 4

mainstream economics *vulgar political economy, orthodox economics* economics taught in schools and colleges based on the trinity formula rather than the law of value 1

manual labour *physical labour* physical labour carried out by a human being 4

manufacture production of commodities using cooperation and the division of labour but few machines 4

market price *selling price* the price at which capitalists sell commodities 12

mass of profit the amount of profit 14

mass of surplus value the amount of surplus value 3

materialised labour see dead labour

means of circulation *medium of circulation* the role money plays in the circulation of commodities 1

means of labour see instrument of labour

means of payment the role money plays when paying a debt 1

means of production *producer goods, conditions of labour* the use values used in production, the material factors of the labour process, including raw materials, auxiliary materials, the instruments of labour, machines and buildings 3

means of subsistence *necessities of life* the use values workers need to consume in order to live, reproduce their labour power and reproduce more workers 2

measure of value money's role as the form that the measure of the socially necessary labour time in commodities must take in a society based on commodity production 1

medium of circulation see means of circulation

merchant capitalist see commercial capitalist

merchant someone who trades in commodities produced by other people 8

merchants' capital capital used by merchants to buy and sell commodities produced by other people 8

metabolism see circulation of matter

metal barrier capital's need to convert commodity capital into money capital measured in gold for the reproduction of capital to continue 16

mode of production the way society produces useful products, including the forces of production and relations of production 8

money capital capital in the form of money 9

money capitalist *financial capitalist, financier* a capitalist who makes a profit by lending money 15

money commodity see money material

money dealing capitalist *money capitalist, money lending capitalist, loan capitalist* a capitalist who makes a profit from dealing in money 15

money material *money commodity* the commodity used as money 1

money of account see measure of value

money *universal equivalent* the commodity that functions as a measure of the value of other commodities, as a standard of price and, by itself or through a symbol, as the medium of circulation 1

monopoly control 8

monopoly price price based solely on the willingness of someone to pay 17

monopoly rent rent based solely on the willingness of someone to pay 17

moral depreciation *functional depreciation, obsolescence* The reduction of a commodity's value caused by comparable commodities being produced with less value 4

moral limit see social limit

national currency token money issued by a country as currency 1

national debt *state debt, public debt* the debt of a nation state 8

national value the value of a commodity in the country it is produced 6

natural form the form something takes in all societies 1

natural limit *physical limit, absolute limit* a limit imposed by nature 2

nature the natural world 1

necessary labour *paid labour* labour that produces value equal to a worker's means of subsistence 3

necessary labour time *paid labour time* the part of the working day during which the worker produces value equal to the value of their wages (not the same as *socially necessary abstract labour time*) 3

necessity what is necessary to survive and reproduce 18

nominal wage the wage paid to a worker 6

object of labour *subject of labour* the parts of nature and products of labour that human beings transform into products during the labour process 3

objectified labour see dead labour

organic composition of capital *composition of capital* the technical composition of capital in value terms 7

original accumulation *original accumulation of capital, primitive accumulation, previous accumulation, original expropriation* the historical process that gives birth to capitalist production by separating producers from the land 8

original capital *capital advanced* money a capitalist invests in labour power and means of production in order to produce commodities and surplus value 3

orthodox economics see mainstream economics

overproduction of capital over accumulation of capital 14

overtime wages paid above the normal wages for a working day for labouring longer 6

paid labour see necessary labour

paid labour time see necessary labour time

past labour see dead labour

peasant a producer working the land to live while paying rent to a landowner 8

petty industry see domestic industry

physical depreciation the reduction of a commodity's value through wear and tear 4

physical limit see natural limit

piece wage a wage that is paid according to the amount of commodities produced 6

potential money capital see reserve fund

price of production see production price

price the amount of money a commodity sells at, the cost of a commodity 1

prime mover see energy source

primitive accumulation see original accumulation

private capital capital owned by individual capitalists 16

private labour labour carried out by an individual or group 1

producer good see intermediate good

producer goods see means of production

producer someone who produces products 1

product *product of labour* a useful thing produced by human beings interacting with other parts of nature 1

production *realisation of labour* the process that creates use values and value 3

production price *price of production, natural price* the price of a commodity when it comprises the cost price of producing commodities plus the average rate of profit 13

production process see labour process

production time the part of the circuit of industrial capital when commodities are in the sphere of production 10

productive capital capital in the process of producing surplus value 9

productive capital see industrial capital

productive consumption the consumption of commodities during the labour process 7

productive labour labour that produces surplus value for a capitalist 5

productive power of capital the appearance that capital produces things that are produced by labour 4

productive power of machines *productivity of machinery* the power machines have to increase the productivity of human labour 4

productive power of nature *productivity of nature, natural wealth* the power non-human nature has to increase the productivity of human labour 4

productive power of science *productivity of science* the power science has to increase the productivity of human labour 4

productive power of social labour *social productive power of labour, productivity of social labour, social powers of labour, collective power of the masses* the power cooperation and the division of labour has to raise the productivity of human labour 4

productive power of society what a society produces 14

productive worker a worker who produces surplus value for a capitalist 5

productivity of labour *productivity, productiveness of labour, productive power of labour, social productiveness of labour* the speed at which a certain amount of labour can produce use values 1

profit a form of surplus value 12

profit equalisation the equalisation of profits between capitalists through competition 13

profit of enterprise profit made by industrial capitalists after they have paid interest on loans and all other costs 16

proletarian see worker

proletariat see working class

protectionism *system of protection, trade protectionism* the restriction of imports from other countries using tariffs, quotas, and other actions by states 8

quantity of money amount of money 1

racism the oppression of black and other oppressed racial groups 13

rate of exchange see exchange rate

rate of exploitation *rate of surplus value* the ratio of surplus value (s) to variable capital (v), s / v 3

rate of interest *interest rate* the percentage rate that interest on a loan is paid at 16

rate of profit *relative increment of capital, rate of self-expansion of capital* the ratio of surplus value (s) to total capital (C), s / C 12

rate of surplus value see rate of exploitation

raw material parts of nature processed by labour to become objects of labour in the labour process 3

real capital see functioning capital

real subsumption the control of the labour process by capitalists using machines that dictate the nature of the labour process 5

real wage what a worker can buy with their wage 6

realisation *selling* turning commodity capital into money capital 9

recession *stagnation, depression, slump* the period in the industrial cycle between crisis and recovery when production is depressed 7

recovery *moderate activity, average activity, expansion* the period in the industrial cycle between recession and boom when production grows 7

relations of production *relations of social production* the relationships between people producing use values 8

relative form of value the form of value a commodity has when expressing its value in the use value of another commodity 1

relative surplus population workers made unemployed by increasing productivity 7

relative surplus value surplus value arising from shortening necessary labour time 4

released capital capital that had to be reconverted into constant and variable capital up to a certain time but is now unnecessary for production to continue on the previous scale 10

rent *ground rent, capitalist ground rent* the part of surplus value paid by capitalists to landowners for the use of land 17

replacement capital see tied up capital

reproduction of capital *capitalist reproduction* the process by which capital continues its existence 7

reproduction on an extended scale see accumulation of capital

reproductive labour see domestic labour

reserve army of labour unemployed workers 7

reserve fund *potential money capital, reserve money capital, latent money capital, sinking fund, accumulation fund, money reserve fund* money capital hoarded by capitalists to pay for future expenditure 9

reserve money capital money capital in excess of what is needed for current production 10

revenue the part of surplus value that capitalists consume themselves rather than reinvest as capital 7

science the collection and organisation of testable knowledge about reality 4

scientific labour see universal labour

self-expansion of capital *valorisation* the growth of capital through the exploitation of labour 3

selling price see market price

selling time the time when capital exists as produced commodities waiting to be sold 10

service a commodity that is consumed at the same time as it is produced 5

share *stock* a share in the ownership of a company 16

simple labour see average labour

simple reproduction *simple reproduction of capital* the reproduction of capital without accumulation, where all surplus value is consumed as revenue 7

sinking fund see reserve fund

skill human ability 1

slavery the ownership of people as property 8

slump see recession

social capital capital owned by shareholders 16

social division of labour see division of labour in society

social form the form something takes in a particular society 1

social labour *direct social labour* labour that forms a part of society's total commodity producing labour 1

social limit *moral limit* a limit imposed by society 2

social value see value

socialised production see collective production

socialised property see collective property

socialism *communism* the common ownership and control of the means of production and distribution by associated producers, introduction

socially necessary abstract labour time *socially necessary labour time, labour time* the amount of abstract labour measured in time that it usually takes to produce a commodity 1

speculation an investment in a risky venture in the hope of surplus profit 16

speculative bubble *economic bubble, financial bubble* the period when speculation causes the price of a commodity, often fictitious capital, to rise unsustainably before crashing 16

sphere of circulation *circulation process, sphere of exchange* the part of the circuit of industrial capital when commodities are bought and sold 9

spheres of production *production process* the part of the circuit of industrial capital when commodities are produced 9

stagnant surplus population see casual workers 7

stagnation see recession

standard of price *unit of account* money's role of allowing commodities to have a price 1

state the collection of institutions that makes and enforces laws within a country 1

stock market *share market, equity market* market places where company shares are traded 16

stock see share

subject of labour see object of labour

subjection see subsumption

subsumption *subjection* the control of the labour process by capital (the category of subsumption is introduced in a draft of part of *Capital* called *Results of the Direct Production Process*) 5

superprofit see surplus profit

supervisor a worker employed to supervise other workers 4

supply chain *commodity supply* system for the circulation of commodities 9

surplus labour time *unpaid labour time* the part of the working day during which workers produce surplus value 3

surplus labour *unpaid labour* labour that produces surplus value for capitalists 3

surplus profit *superprofit* profit above the average profit 13

surplus value the value workers produce for capitalists above the value of their wages 3

taxation money collected by states to fund the running of the state 8

technical composition of capital *physical composition of capital* the ratio between the amount of dead labour and living labour in the labour process 7

technology the application of science 4

tied up capital *replacement capital* capital that must be reconverted into constant and variable capital if production is to proceed on the same scale 10

time wage wages paid according to the time worked 6

token money anything that represents money in exchange but is not the money material 1

total annual product *annual product, annual commodity product* the total product of a society in a year 11

total capital the amount of capital in an individual capital 12

total social capital *total capital, aggregate social capital* the total of all individual capitals, capital as a whole 11

trade cycle see industrial cycle

trade war see commercial war

trading capital see commercial capital

trading capitalist see commercial capitalist

transfer pricing the deflation and inflation of costs in different countries by corporations 13

trinity formula the view of mainstream economics that profit, rent and wages are fair payment for the factors of production 18

turnover time *turnover period* the time it takes a capital to complete a turnover 10

turnover *turnover of capital, circuit of capital* the completion of the circulation of capital from investment to the return of more money 10

underconsumptionism the view that capitalist crises are caused by wages being too low 11

unequal exchange the transfer of surplus value produced by workers in lower productivity countries to capitalists in high productivity countries through international trade 6

universal equivalent the commodity with the use value that other commodities express their value in 1

universal labour *scientific labour* intellectual labour that advances science 4

universal money see world money

unpaid labour see surplus labour

unpaid labour time see surplus labour time

unproductive labour labour for a capitalist that does not produce surplus value 5

unproductive worker a worker who is paid from surplus value to carry out unproductive labour 5

use value the ability to satisfy a human need or want 1

useful labour see concrete labour

usurer money lender 8

usurers' capital capital owned by a usurer 8

valorisation see capitalist production and self-expansion of capital

value composition of capital the ratio between capital invested in constant capital and variable capital 7

value form see exchange value

value of labour power the value of the commodities forming the worker's means of subsistence 2

value *real value, social value (as opposed to individual value* the quality of being the product of social labour 1

variable capital capital invested in labour power that reproduces its own value as well as producing surplus value during the labour process 3

vulgar political economy see mainstream economics

wage labourer see worker

wage money paid to workers by capitalists in return for the use of their labour power 6

wage slavery see capitalist relationship

wage worker see worker

wages of management *wages of supervision, wages of superintendence* wages paid by capitalists to managers to run companies for them 16

waiting time *excess production time* the time when commodities are in the sphere of production but not in the labour process 10

wealth an abundance of useful things 1

women's oppression the oppression of women in society 2

worker *labourer, free labourer, wage labourer, wage worker, proletarian* someone who exists by selling their labour power to a capitalist in return for wages 2

working class *proletariat* the class in capitalist society that has to sell its labour power to capitalists to exist 3

working day the time during which workers engage in the labour process each day 3 working period see labour time

world market trade in commodities between countries 1

world money *money of the world, money as money, universal money* the materialisation of social wealth and universal means of payment, gold 1

References

Introduction
1 *Letter to Engels*, Karl Marx, 31st July 1865
2 *World on brink of five 'disastrous' climate tipping points, study finds* Damian Carrington, the Guardian, 8th September 2022
3 *Capital,* Karl Marx, Marxists Internet Archive
4 *Capitalism Seen Doing 'More Harm than Good' in Global Survey*, Mark John, Reuters, 19th January 2020

1 Commodities and money
1 World Population Review
2 World Population Review
3 *World military expenditure reaches new record high as European spending surges*, Stockholm International Peace Research Institute
4 Country Cassette
5 *As good as gold*, Adam Tooze, New Statesman, 13th October 2022
6 *A Contribution to the Critique of Political Economy*, Karl Marx, 1859
7 *The Theory of Political Economy*, William Stanley Jevons, 1871

4 Productivity

1 *Less is More,* Jason Hickel, 2020, page 29
2 *Less is More,* Jason Hickel, 2020, page 99
3 *Global inequalities in CO2 emissions,* Our World in Data
4 *The Human Planet: How We Created the Anthropocene,* Simon Lewis and Mark A Maslin, 2018

7 Accumulation

1 *Less is more,* Jason Hickel, 2020, page 90
2 Our World in Data
3 *The Violent Crackup of the Post-WWII International Order: Notes on the Geopolitical Crisis and Global Capital,* William I Robinson, 27th March 2023
4 *Paper Straws Are Not Enough. Only "System Change" Can Halt Climate Crisis, Says George Monbiot,* Democracy Now!
5 *Addendum: 1% of all adults in the world own 44.5% of all personal wealth, while more than 52% have only 1.2%,* Michael Roberts, 2023
6 *Survival of the Richest: How we must tax the super-rich now to fight inequality,* Oxfam

13 Competition

1 *Imperialism and the development myth: How rich countries dominate in the twenty-first century,* part 1, Sam King, 2021
2 *Imperialist appropriation in the world economy: Drain from the global South through unequal exchange, 1990–2015,* Jason Hickel, Christian Dorninger, Hanspeter Wieland and Intan Suwandi, Global Environmental Change, Volume 73, March 2022
3 *The economic impact of colonialism,* Daron Acemoglu, 30th January 2017

4 *HM2 – The economics of modern imperialism,* Michael Roberts, 14th November 2019

5 *Marx 200: A review of Marx's economics 200 years after his birth,* chapter 5, Michael Roberts, 2018

14 The falling rate of profit

1 The Economist, 26th January 2019, quoted in *Can Global Capitalism Endure?* William I Robinson, 6th November 2021

2 *A world rate of profit: important new evidence,* Michael Roberts blog, blogging from a Marxist economist, 22nd January 2022

16 Interest and fictitious capital

1 *Tulip Mania* at Wikipedia

2 *Global public debt hits record $92 trillion, UN report says,* Jorgelina Do Rosario, Reuters, 12th July 2023

3 *What does 'global debt' mean and how high is it now?,* Victoria Masterson, 16th May 2022

4 World Bank

5 *Can Global Capitalism Endure?* William I Robinson, 6th November 2021

6 *Crushing' debt crisis spells development disaster for billions,* United Nations, 12th July 2023

7 *Global public debt hits record $92 trillion, UN report says,* Jorgelina Do Rosario, Reuters, 12th July 2023

8 *Debt Service Payments Put Biggest Squeeze on Poor Countries Since 2000,* World Bank, 6th December 2022

Printed in Great Britain
by Amazon